KICKSTART YOUR WELLNESS WITH ANTI-INFLAMMATORY DIET FOR BEGINNERS:

Full-Color Cookbook with 2000 Days of Easy to Cook Recipes to Reduce Inflammation.
28-Day Meal Plan to Boost Immune System & Health

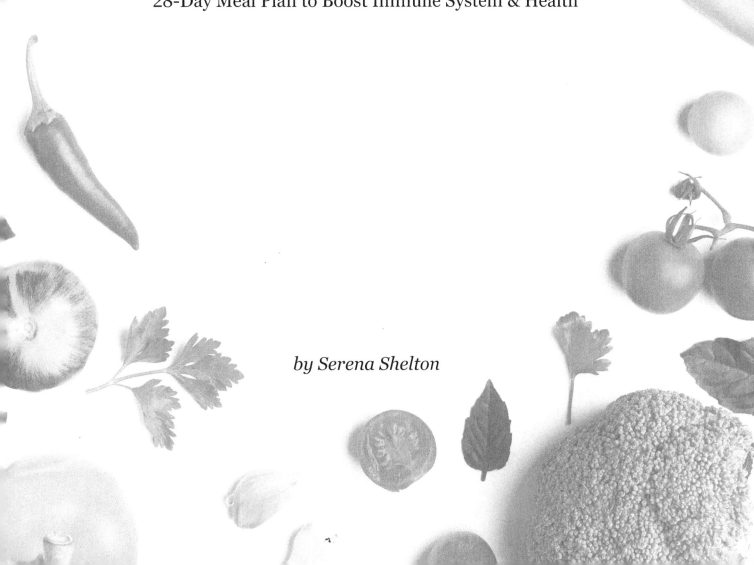

by Serena Shelton

Legal Disclaimer

The recipes and culinary advice presented in this cookbook have been carefully developed and tested by the author, who is a professional chef. However, the author cannot guarantee the results of the recipes for all individuals, as variations in cooking techniques, ingredient quality, and individual tastes may affect the outcome.
The information provided in this cookbook is for general informational purposes and is not intended as professional culinary or dietary advice. Use your best judgment and exercise caution when handling and preparing ingredients, particularly if you have food allergies, dietary restrictions, or other health concerns.

The author disclaims any liability for any injuries, losses, or damages resulting from using or misusing the information and recipes presented in this cookbook. Cooking involves inherent risks, and readers are responsible for following proper safety precautions and guidelines when working in the kitchen.

Please be aware that nutritional information provided with the recipes is an estimate and may vary based on ingredient substitutions and portion sizes. For accurate dietary information, it is recommended to consult with a registered dietitian or nutritionist.
The recipes in this cookbook are intended for personal use and enjoyment. Any commercial use or distribution of the content without the author's written consent is strictly prohibited.

ISBN: 979-8857566107

Published by AT & AN Publishing
For permission requests or inquiries, please contact the author at atanoblepublishing@gmail.com

The table of

CONTENTS

INTRODUCTION

Welcome to "Kickstart Your Wellness with Anti-Inflammatory Diet for Beginners: Full-Color Cookbook with 2000 Days of Easy-to-Cook Recipes to Reduce Inflammation. 28-Day Meal Plan to Boost Immune System & Health".

Whether you're starting your journey towards improved well-being or seeking a holistic approach to wellness, this book is your essential guide to harnessing the power of an anti-inflammatory diet.

In the following pages, you'll find a wealth of information, expertly curated recipes, and practical resources designed to empower you on your path to vibrant health. As an experienced writer, dietician, chef, and nutrition expert, I've poured my knowledge and passion into crafting a book that is as informative as it is flavorful.

In "Kickstart Your Wellness," we delve deep into the anti-inflammatory diet principles, demystifying the intricate connection between diet and inflammation. You'll understand how inflammation impacts your health and discover how this diet can be a potent tool in your journey to a healthier you. From understanding pantry staples to selecting the right kitchen tools, we've got you covered to set you up for success.

The heart of this book lies in its collection of 2,000 days' worth of recipes. From energizing breakfasts to satisfying snacks, vibrant salads, and delectable desserts, each recipe is carefully crafted to include ingredients that are easy to find in stores. No more guessing what's suitable for your body – our 28-day meal plan takes the guesswork out of meal prep, ensuring a seamless transition into a new way of eating.

Whether tackling chronic inflammation, seeking relief from joint pain, aiming to manage your weight, or simply striving for overall wellness, this book caters to a diverse range of needs. Our recipes not only tantalize your taste buds but are also designed to combat inflammation and promote better health. With dishes that burst with flavor and nutrition, you'll be excited to explore a new world of culinary delights that support your well-being.

This book is more than just a cookbook – it's your steadfast companion on your wellness journey. It's a comprehensive resource for health-conscious individuals, fitness enthusiasts, parents, and anyone looking to enhance their quality of life. By embracing the principles within these pages, you're embarking on a transformative journey toward improved energy, vitality, and longevity.

So, flip through these pages, immerse yourself in the colorful array of recipes, and let the aroma of health and well-being fill your kitchen. You're moving towards a healthier, happier you with each recipe you create. Welcome to a world where deliciousness and wellness coexist – let's kickstart your journey to a life of vitality and vibrant health!

EVERYTHING YOU NEED TO KNOW ABOUT

Anti-Inflammatory Diet

Understanding Inflammation and its Impact on Health

Inflammation is a natural and vital process in the body as a defense mechanism against harmful stimuli such as infections, injuries, and toxins. When you cut your finger, the area becomes inflamed as your immune system sends an army of white blood cells to protect against potential pathogens and initiate healing. In acute situations like this, inflammation is a protective response that aids in the body's recovery.

However, chronic inflammation is a different story. It is a persistent and low-grade form of inflammation that can silently wreak havoc on your health. Unlike acute inflammation, which is short-lived and beneficial, chronic inflammation can cause various health issues, contributing to multiple diseases, including cardiovascular disease, type 2 diabetes, arthritis, and certain cancers.

The modern Western diet, characterized by high consumption of processed foods, refined sugars, unhealthy fats, and artificial additives, has been closely linked to chronic inflammation. This type of diet can trigger the immune system to be in a constant state of alertness, leading to the release of pro-inflammatory chemicals.

Fortunately, we can influence inflammation through the foods we choose to eat. The Anti-Inflammatory Diet is a dietary approach designed to help reduce inflammation, promote overall well-being, and support optimal health. By being conscious of the foods we consume, we can work towards calming the flames of inflammation and nurturing our bodies back to balance.

In this cookbook, we will delve into the principles of the Anti-Inflammatory Diet and provide you with a diverse array of delicious and nourishing recipes to help you embark on this journey to whole-body wellness. Each recipe has been thoughtfully crafted to include ingredients known for their anti-inflammatory properties,

such as colorful fruits and vegetables, healthy fats like omega-3 fatty acids, herbs, spices, and lean proteins.

As you explore the recipes and incorporate them into your daily meals, you'll discover a world of flavors and textures and experience the potential benefits of reduced inflammation, improved digestion, enhanced energy levels, and better overall health.

Before you dive into the recipes, we encourage you to take the time to understand the impact of inflammation on your health. By gaining insights into the relationship between diet and inflammation, you'll be better equipped to make informed choices and set yourself on the path to a vibrant and thriving life.

In the following chapters, we will explore energizing breakfasts, wholesome lunches, nourishing dinners, satisfying snacks, comforting soups and stews, seafood delights, and delectable desserts, all centered around the principles of the Anti-Inflammatory Diet. Furthermore, we shall offer guidance and materials to aid you in sustaining this way of eating and embracing an anti-inflammatory lifestyle beyond the kitchen.

Let's embark on this journey together, empowering ourselves with knowledge, making conscious food choices, and savoring the goodness from nourishing our bodies with foods promoting well-being and vitality. Let's step towards reducing inflammation and unlocking the potential for a healthier and happier life.

The Connection Between Diet and Inflammation

In recent years, scientific research has shed significant light on the relationship between diet and inflammation, highlighting the profound impact that food choices can have on our body's inflammatory response. The foods we consume can fuel the inflammation process or act as powerful allies in reducing it. Understanding this connection is crucial in our quest for improved health and well-being.

Some foods, like processed and sugary items and unhealthy fats in fast food and processed snacks, have been identified as pro-inflammatory. When regularly consumed, these foods can trigger the release of pro-inflammatory molecules, leading to chronic low-grade inflammation. Over time, this chronic inflammation can contribute to the development and progression of diverse chronic diseases, including but not limited to heart diseases, diabetes, obesity, and autoimmune conditions.

On the other hand, an anti-inflammatory diet rich in whole, unprocessed foods provides the body with abundant nutrients, antioxidants, and anti-inflammatory compounds that can help quell inflammation and support overall health. Fruits and vegetables, mainly those vibrant in color, are rich with antioxidants like vitamins C and E, which neutralize free radicals and reduce oxidative stress that can promote inflammation.

Incorporating foods high in omega-3 fatty acids, like fatty fish, flaxseeds, and chia seeds, can improve and offset the body's pro-inflammatory omega-6 fatty acids ratio to anti-inflammatory omega-3s. These healthy fats have been reported to reduce inflammation and support cardiovascular health.

Herbs and spices like turmeric, ginger, garlic, and cinnamon contain potent anti-inflammatory compounds that can modulate the body's inflammatory response. Including these flavor-packed ingredients in your meals can add not only taste but also a myriad of health benefits.

Whole grains, legumes, nuts, and seeds are rich in fiber and plant-based compounds that promote a healthy gut microbiome. A balanced and diverse gut microbiome is associated with reduced inflammation and improved immune function.

Furthermore, it is essential to consider individual food sensitivities and intolerances. Certain foods can trigger inflammation in some people, even if they are generally considered healthy. Identifying and eliminating these trigger foods can be instrumental in reducing chronic inflammation.

By recognizing the direct connection between diet and inflammation, we can take proactive steps to optimize our health. Embracing an anti-inflammatory diet can provide our bodies with the tools to combat inflammation, improve immune function, and support overall wellness.

Throughout this cookbook, we have carefully curated recipes emphasizing anti-inflammatory ingredients, allowing you to savor flavorful dishes while nurturing your body. As you start your culinary adventure, remember that small, consistent changes in your eating habits can significantly improve your health and well-being. Let food be your ally in the battle against inflammation as you explore the nourishing and delicious recipes we have prepared for you.

Benefits of the Anti-Inflammatory Diet

The Anti-Inflammatory Diet offers a myriad of benefits that extend far beyond simply reducing inflammation. By embracing this dietary approach, you can experience positive transformations in your health and well-being.

Here are some of the notable benefits of adopting an anti-inflammatory lifestyle:

- **Reduced Inflammation:** The primary objective of the Anti-Inflammatory Diet is to minimize chronic inflammation in the body. By consuming foods with anti-inflammatory properties, you can help balance the body's inflammatory response, potentially reducing the risk of inflammation-related chronic diseases.
- **Enhanced Heart Health:** An anti-inflammatory diet can positively impact heart health by promoting a healthy cardiovascular system. Eating foods like fatty fish are rich in omega-3 fatty acids, fiber-rich whole grains, and antioxidant-packed fruits and vegetables, can support heart function and reduce the risk of heart disease.
- **Better Digestive Health:** The abundance of fiber in an anti-inflammatory diet supports a healthy gut environment and promotes regular bowel movements. A well-functioning gut can improve nutrient absorption, enhance digestion, and reduce discomfort.
- **Weight Management:** Adopting an anti-inflammatory lifestyle can aid weight management and loss. Whole, nutrient-dense foods can help control hunger and cravings, making keeping a healthy and comfortable weight easier.
- **Improved Energy Levels:** Nourishing your body with nutrient-rich foods provides a sustainable energy source throughout the day. Avoiding processed and sugary foods can prevent energy crashes and provide a steady vitality supply.
- **Enhanced Brain Function:** The Anti-Inflammatory Diet's focus on antioxidant-rich foods supports brain health and cognitive function. Antioxidants are beneficial in safeguarding brain cells against oxidative stress and may lower the chances of cognitive decline that comes with aging.
- **Balanced Blood Sugar Levels:** An anti-inflammatory diet can help stabilize blood sugar levels by avoiding high-sugar and refined carbohydrate foods. This diet can also benefit individuals with or at risk of type 2 diabetes.
- **Joint Health:** Many individuals with inflammatory conditions such as arthritis have reported improved joint pain and inflammation by following an anti-inflammatory diet. Certain foods, like fatty fish and turmeric, possess anti-inflammatory properties that can benefit joint health.
- **Skin Health:** Antioxidant-rich foods found in the Anti-Inflammatory Diet can promote healthy skin by protecting it from free radical damage and supporting collagen production.
- **Enhanced Immune Function:** A well-balanced, nutrient-rich diet can bolster the immune system, providing better protection against infections and illnesses.
- **Reduced Risk of Chronic Diseases:** Studies have connected chronic inflammation to numerous diseases, including diabetes, obesity, cancer, and autoimmune conditions. Addressing inflammation through diet may reduce the risk of these diseases.
- **Overall Well-Being:** Embracing an anti-inflammatory lifestyle fosters a sense of well-being, as the focus shifts towards nourishing the body with wholesome foods and promoting optimal health.

As you explore the recipes in this cookbook and integrate the principles of the Anti-Inflammatory Diet into your daily life, you can reap these advantages and experience a positive impact on your health and vitality. It's essential to remember that every effort made towards a healthier diet is a step towards a healthier version of yourself.

Essential Tips for Embarking on an Anti-Inflammatory Journey

Congratulations on taking the first step toward embracing an anti-inflammatory lifestyle!

Transitioning to an anti-inflammatory diet can be a transformative journey that empowers you to take charge of your health and well-being. To set yourself up for success, here are some essential tips to guide you on this path:

- **Educate Yourself:** Knowledge is power. Take the time to educate yourself about inflammation, the impact of diet on inflammation, and the principles of the Anti-Inflammatory Diet. Understanding the science behind it will reinforce your commitment and help you make informed food choices.
- **Start Gradually:** Drastically changing your diet overnight can be overwhelming and unsustainable. Instead, ease into the anti-inflammatory lifestyle by incorporating one or two new recipes or food choices each week. Gradual changes are more likely to become lasting habits.
- **Focus on Whole Foods:** Base your meals around whole, unprocessed foods. Fresh fruits, vegetables, whole grains, lean proteins, nuts, and seeds should become the backbone of your anti-inflammatory diet. Minimize or eliminate processed and refined foods, as they can promote inflammation.
- **Colorful Plate:** Aim to have a colorful plate with various fruits and vegetables. The vibrant colors indicate an abundance of antioxidants and phytonutrients that can combat inflammation and support overall health.
- **Healthy Fats:** Include sources of healthy fats in your diet: avocados, olive oil, nuts, and fatty fish. These fats contain omega-3 fatty acids, which possess anti-inflammatory properties.
- **Spice it Up:** Herbs and spices like turmeric, ginger, garlic, and cinnamon not only add depth of flavor to your meals but also offer powerful anti-inflammatory benefits — experiment with incorporating them into your dishes.
- **Hydration:** Stay well-hydrated by consuming plenty of water throughout the day. Water is essential for the body's proper functioning and can aid in reducing inflammation.
- **Mindful Eating:** Pay attention to how you feel before, during, and after meals. Mindful eating can help you recognize how different foods affect your body and identify potential food sensitivities.
- **Meal Planning:** Plan your meals beforehand to ensure you have the necessary ingredients and avoid impulsive food choices that may not align with the anti-inflammatory diet.
- **Read Labels:** When purchasing packaged foods, read the labels carefully. Avoid buying products with added sugars, unhealthy fats, and artificial additives.
- **Listen to Your Body:** Every individual's response to food is unique. Pay attention to how your body reacts to certain foods and adjust your diet accordingly. Keep a food journal to track any changes in symptoms or well-being.
- **Be Patient and Flexible:**
  1. It is essential to keep in mind that changing your eating habits requires both time and patience.
  2. Be kind to yourself and celebrate your progress. If you slip up or face challenges, don't be discouraged.
  3. Approach the journey with a flexible mindset, and know that every positive choice you make is a step in the right direction.
- **Seek Support:** Share your anti-inflammatory journey with friends, family, or online communities. Having support and encouragement can make the transition more enjoyable and motivating.

Following these essential tips can lay a strong foundation for your anti-inflammatory journey. Embrace the process with an open mind and a willingness to explore unique flavors and cuisines. Remember, this is not a restrictive diet but a nourishing and delicious lifestyle leading to improved health and vitality. As you embark on this transformative path, be gentle with yourself, stay curious, and enjoy the nourishing benefits of each mouthwatering bite.

Pantry Staples and Kitchen Tools for Success

In the heart of every culinary adventure lies a well-stocked pantry and an arsenal of kitchen tools that form the backbone of creative and nourishing cooking. As you embark on your anti-inflammatory journey, ensuring that your kitchen is equipped with essential ingredients and tools will empower you to embrace this lifestyle change enthusiastically and confidently.

Pantry Staples: Your Foundation for Flavorful Creations

Building a pantry tailored to the anti-inflammatory diet is akin to laying a solid foundation for a sturdy house. These staples will be your go-to ingredients, allowing you to craft various mouthwatering dishes while supporting your wellness goals. Here's a closer look at these pantry superheroes:

1. **Whole Grains:** Whole grains are the backbone of many balanced meals. Stock your pantry with brown rice, quinoa, oats, and whole wheat pasta. Their complex carbohydrates provide sustained energy while essential nutrients nourish your body from within.

2. **Healthy Oils:** The choice of cooking oil can significantly influence both flavor and health benefits. Extra-virgin olive oil takes center stage for its robust flavor and wealth of monounsaturated fats, known to promote heart health and reduce inflammation. For higher-temperature cooking, consider avocado oil with its high smoke point.

3. **Herbs and Spices:** An assortment of herbs and spices transforms ordinary dishes into culinary masterpieces. Turmeric, revered for its anti-inflammatory compound curcumin, takes a leading role. Embrace the warmth of ginger, the aroma of garlic, the freshness of basil, and the complexity of oregano to elevate your recipes.

4. **Canned Tomatoes:** Canned tomatoes are a universal addition to your pantry, contributing to sauces, stews, soups, and more. They offer lycopene, a powerful antioxidant known to combat inflammation and support heart health.

5. **Legumes:** Lentils, chickpeas, black beans, and kidney beans are champions of plant-based protein and dietary fiber. These legumes provide sustenance and aid in stabilizing blood sugar levels and promoting digestive health.

6. **Nuts and Seeds:** Almonds, walnuts, chia seeds, and flaxseeds bring a delightful crunch and a dose of healthy fats to your meals. Incorporate them into breakfasts, snacks, and salads for added texture and nutrition.

7. **Nut Butter:** Natural nut butter offers a spreadable protein source and healthy fats.

8. **Whole Grain Flour:** For moments of baking inspiration, having whole grain flour like whole wheat or almond flour allows you to create delectable treats without sacrificing nutritional value.

9. **Condiments:** Elevate your dishes with sophistication using condiments like balsamic vinegar, tamari (a gluten-free soy sauce alternative), and Dijon mustard. These add depth and complexity to your culinary creations.

Kitchen Tools: Your Culinary Allies

Equipping your kitchen with the right tools ensures that your cooking experience is efficient, enjoyable, and productive. Here's a glimpse into the kitchen tools that will be your trusty companions on this anti-inflammatory journey:

1. **Chef's Knife:** The cornerstone of culinary prowess, a sharp chef's knife simplifies slicing, dicing, and chopping tasks. Invest in a high-quality knife that fits comfortably in your hand.

2. **Cutting Boards:** Prevent cross-contamination using separate cutting boards for different food groups. This practice maintains food safety and hygiene.

3. **Food Processor or Blender:** These versatile appliances lend their power to create silky smoothies, creamy sauces, and wholesome dips. They're your allies in turning raw ingredients into culinary marvels.

4. **Non-Stick Cookware:** Non-stick pots and pans coated with ceramic make cooking with minimal oil a breeze, ensuring that your meals retain their healthful essence.

5. **Baking Sheets:** Whether roasting vegetables or baking proteins, these sheets become your canvases for creating vibrant and delicious dishes.

6. **Measuring Tools:** Accurate measurements are the secret to consistent results. Invest in measuring cups and spoons to ensure precision in your culinary endeavors.

7. **Mixing Bowls:** From tossing salads to mixing

ingredients, an assortment of mixing bowls in varying sizes supports your culinary creativity.

8. **Storage Containers:** Preserve your culinary triumphs with storage containers that keep your meals fresh and ready for future indulgence.

Transform your kitchen into a culinary sanctuary by exploring the art of ingredient and tool pairing. Make mindful choices that lead to nourishing cuisine, and enjoy the magic that unfolds on your anti-inflammatory journey.

Unveiling the Ingredients: Your Allies and Adversaries

As you embark on your anti-inflammatory diet, it's crucial to understand the ingredients that will elevate your well-being. Let's explore these heroes:

- **Fruits and Vegetables:** Berries, cherries, oranges, apples, avocados, and pineapples grace your plate with their vibrant colors and powerful antioxidants. Leafy greens like spinach and kale, cruciferous vegetables such as broccoli and cauliflower, and the sweetness of bell peppers and tomatoes are your allies in the fight against inflammation.
- **Whole Grains:** Nourish your body with the wholesome goodness of brown rice, quinoa, oats, and whole wheat bread. These grains provide sustained energy and essential nutrients to your overall well-being.
- **Healthy Fats:** Harness the benefits of extra-virgin olive oil, avocados, almonds, walnuts, and flaxseeds. These sources of healthy fats enhance your dishes' flavor, support heart health, and reduce inflammation.
- **Fatty Fish:** Salmon, mackerel, sardines, and trout are your aquatic allies, rich in omega-3 fatty acids with potent anti-inflammatory properties.
- **Legumes:** Lentils, chickpeas, black beans, and kidney beans offer a plant-based protein source packed with fiber and nutrients, contributing to stable blood sugar levels and reducing inflammation.
- **Herbs and Spices:** Embrace the aromatic power of turmeric, ginger, garlic, basil, and oregano. These herbs and spices enliven your dishes and offer compounds that combat inflammation.

- **Teas:** Green, chamomile, and ginger tea provide a soothing and hydrating way to enjoy anti-inflammatory compounds.
- **Dark Chocolate:** Savor the indulgence of dark chocolate (70% cocoa content or higher) in moderation, relishing its antioxidant-rich properties.
- **Probiotic Foods:** Elevate your gut health with yogurt (with live cultures), kefir, sauerkraut, and kimchi, contributing to a balanced and thriving microbiome.

Avoiding ingredients that can trigger inflammation and undermine your well-being is essential. Keep off your plate the following list:
- **Processed Foods:** Bid farewell to fast foods, frozen meals, and packaged snacks often loaded with unhealthy fats, sugars, and additives.
- **Refined Grains:** Leave behind white bread, white rice, and regular pasta that lack the nutrients and fiber in whole grains.
- **Sugary Foods:** Say no to sodas, candies, pastries, and desserts high in added sugars, as they contribute to inflammation and disrupt your body's equilibrium.
- **Trans Fats:** Steer clear of partially hydrogenated oils in fried foods and specific packaged snacks, as they promote inflammation and risk heart health.
- **Highly Processed Meats:** Opt for alternatives to processed meats like sausages, bacon, and hot dogs, which can trigger inflammation and harm your health.
- **Vegetable Oils:** Skip corn oil, sunflower oil, and soybean oil, opting instead for healthier alternatives like olive oil and avocado oil.
- **Artificial Sweeteners:** Avoid aspartame, sucralose, and saccharin, commonly found in diet sodas and low-calorie sweeteners, as they may disrupt your body's natural processes.
- **Highly Refined Snack Foods:** Pass up on chips, crackers, and other snacks made with refined ingredients and unhealthy fats, which can significantly contribute to inflammation and negatively impact your health.
- **Alcohol:** While an occasional indulgence might be considered, limiting alcohol intake is wise as excessive consumption can lead to inflammation and health issue

ENERGIZING

Breakfasts

Begin your day with vitality and nourishment through these delightful Rise-and-Shine Overnight Oats. A blend of wholesome oats, vibrant berries, and nutrient-rich seeds, this breakfast is a breeze to prepare and ensures sustained energy throughout your morning.

RISE-AND-SHINE OVERNIGHT OATS

✓ Servings: 2   ✓ Preparation time: 10 min   ✓ Cooking time: 0 min
                       (plus overnight soaking)

- 1 cup old-fashioned rolled oats
- 1 cup unsweetened almond milk (or preferred plant-based milk)
- 1/2 cup mixed berries (blueberries, raspberries, strawberries)
- 2 tablespoons chia seeds
- 1/2 teaspoon vanilla extract

- 2 tablespoons chopped almonds or walnuts
- 1 tablespoon pure maple syrup (optional for sweetness)
- Pinch of cinnamon
- Small pinch of salt

1. Combine the rolled oats, almond milk, chia seeds, vanilla extract, and a pinch of salt in a mixing bowl. Mix well to ensure thorough integration.
2. Cover the bowl with plastic wrap or a lid and refrigerate overnight (at least 6-8 hours) to allow oats and chia seeds to absorb liquid and thicken.
3. In the morning, gently stir the oat mixture to loosen it. Add a splash of almond milk if a creamier texture is preferred.
4. Fold in the mixed berries, chopped almonds or walnuts, and a pinch of cinnamon. If desired, drizzle pure maple syrup over oats and mix.
5. Divide your Overnight Oats into two serving bowls or jars.
6. Enjoy the oats straight from the fridge, or let them rest at room temperature briefly for a less chilled experience.
7. Enhance the presentation and flavor by garnishing with extra berries, nuts, or a sprinkle of cinnamon.

RECIPE TIP: Customize the flavor and texture by experimenting with various combinations of berries, nuts, and seeds. To plan ahead, double the ingredients and portion the Rise-and-Shine Overnight Oats into individual jars for a week's worth of convenient breakfasts.

SUBSTITUTION TIP: Opt for plant-based yogurt or coconut yogurt instead of dairy milk for a vegan-friendly adaptation

NUTRITIONAL INFORMATION PER SERVING: Calories: 320; Total Fat: 13g; Total Cholesterol: 0mg; Sugar: 7g; Fiber: 10g; Protein: 9g; Sodium: 70mg; Potassium: 380mg

Feel vibrant notes with Berry Bliss Anti-Inflammatory Smoothie Bowls. These bowls are filled with antioxidant-rich berries and nourishing ingredients, making them a refreshing and wholesome breakfast supporting your wellness journey.

BERRY BLISS ANTI-INFLAMMATORY SMOOTHIE BOWLS

 Servings: 2   Preparation time: 10 min   Cooking time: 0 min

- 1 cup mixed berries (blueberries, raspberries, strawberries)
- 1 ripe banana, frozen and sliced
- 1/2 cup unsweetened plant-based milk (consider almond milk)
- 1/2 cup plain Greek yogurt
- 2 tablespoons chia seeds
- 1 tablespoon flaxseeds
- 1 teaspoon pure maple syrup or honey (optional)
- 1/2 teaspoon ground turmeric
- 1/2 teaspoon grated ginger
- A pinch of black pepper (enhancing the turmeric absorption)
- Toppings: Sliced fresh berries, chopped nuts, coconut flakes

1. In a blender, combine the mixed berries, frozen banana slices, almond milk, Greek yogurt, chia seeds, flaxseeds, honey or maple syrup (if using), ground turmeric, grated ginger, and a pinch of black pepper.
2. Blend the mixture at high speed until it becomes smooth and creamy. Add more milk to reach your desired thickness if the consistency is too thick.
3. Taste the smoothie and adjust sweetness by adding more honey or maple syrup if needed.
4. Pour the smoothie into two bowls.
5. Top the bowls with sliced fresh berries, chopped nuts, and coconut flakes to add texture, flavor, and extra nutrition.
6. Serve immediately and enjoy the refreshing and nourishing Berry Bliss Anti-Inflammatory Smoothie Bowls.

RECIPE TIP: Get creative with your toppings! Add a granola sprinkle, nut butter, or a few extra berries to customize your smoothie bowl.

SUBSTITUTION TIP:
- Vegan Variation: Use dairy-free yogurt such as coconut yogurt or almond yogurt instead of Greek yogurt for a vegan-friendly version.
- Nut-Free Option: If you have nut allergies, omit the chopped nuts or replace them with toasted seeds like pumpkin or sunflower seeds.

NUTRITIONAL INFORMATION PER SERVING: Calories: 230; Total Fat: 9g; Total Cholesterol: 0mg; Sugar: 14g; Fiber: 10g; Protein: 9g; Sodium: 45mg; Potassium: 400mg

What a burst of flavor and energy! Our Berry-Licious Chia Seed Pudding combines the goodness of chia seeds, berries, and a touch of sweetness in a creamy and nutritious breakfast.

BERRY-LICIOUS CHIA SEED PUDDING

✔ Servings: 2   ✔ Preparation time: 10 min (plus overnight chilling)   ✔ Cooking time: 0 min

- 1/4 cup chia seeds
- 1 cup unsweetened almond milk (or any preferred milk)
- 1 tablespoon pure maple syrup (adjust to taste)
- - 1/2 teaspoon pure vanilla extract
- 1/2 cup mixed berries (blueberries, raspberries, strawberries)
- 1 tablespoon chopped almonds or walnuts (optional for topping)
- Fresh mint leaves, for garnish (optional)

1. Combine chia seeds, unsweetened almond milk, pure vanilla extract, and maple syrup in a bowl. Whisk the mixture well to ensure the chia seeds are evenly distributed.
2. Allow the mixture to rest for 10 minutes, then whisk again to prevent clumping. Cover the bowl containing the chia seeds and liquid for a pudding-like consistency, and refrigerate it overnight or for at least 4 hours.
3. Give the chia seed pudding a good stir to break up clumps before serving. If the pudding is too thick, just add a splash of almond milk to achieve the desired consistency.
4. Divide the chia seed pudding into serving glasses or bowls.
5. Top the pudding with mixed berries, arranging them evenly over the surface.
6. If desired, sprinkle chopped almonds or walnuts on top for added crunch and healthy fats.
7. Garnish with fresh mint leaves for freshness and color.
8. Serve the Berry-Licious Chia Seed Pudding chilled, and savor the delightful mix of flavors and textures.

RECIPE TIP: Depending on your preference, You can customize this chia seed pudding by using different types of milk, such as coconut or oat milk.

SUBSTITUTION TIP:
- Vegan Variation: Use plant-based milk (such as almond milk, coconut milk, or oat milk) and swap the honey for pure maple syrup or agave syrup.
- Feel free to use your favorite fruits as toppings, such as sliced bananas, kiwi, or mango, to create your unique combination.

NUTRITIONAL INFORMATION PER SERVING: Calories: 180; Total Fat: 8g; Total Cholesterol: 0g; Sugar: 10g; Fiber: 11g; Protein: 5g; Sodium: 60mg; Potassium: 250mg

Begin your day with vitality and nourishment through these delightful Rise-and-Shine Overnight Oats. A blend of wholesome oats, vibrant berries, and nutrient-rich seeds, this breakfast is a breeze to prepare and ensures sustained energy throughout your morning.

SAVORY SPINACH AND SWEET POTATO FRITTATA

 Servings: 4   Preparation time: 15 min   Cooking time: 30 min

- 1 medium sweet potato, peeled and thinly sliced
- 2 tablespoons extra-virgin olive oil
- 1 cup baby spinach, chopped
- 1/2 red bell pepper, diced
- 1/4 red onion, finely chopped
- 6 large eggs

- 1/4 cup almond milk (or any unsweetened plant-based milk)
- 1 teaspoon dried oregano
- 1/2 teaspoon garlic powder
- Salt and pepper to taste
- 1/4 cup grated dairy-free cheese (optional)
- Fresh parsley, chopped, for garnish

1. Preheat your oven to 375°F (190°C).
2. Heat a tablespoon of olive oil over medium heat in a big oven-safe skillet. Add the thinly sliced sweet potato and cook for about 5-7 minutes, occasionally flipping, until the sweet potato slices are slightly softened and golden brown. Take the food out of the pan and put it to the side.
3. Dispense the remaining tablespoon of olive oil into the same skillet. Add the chopped red bell pepper and diced red onion. Sauté for about 3-4 minutes until the vegetables are tender.
4. Add the chopped baby spinach to the mixture and cook it for 1-2 minutes until it is completely wilted. Remove from heat.
5. Whisk the eggs, almond milk, garlic powder, salt, dried oregano, and pepper in a mixing bowl.
6. Arrange the cooked sweet potato slices in the bottom of the skillet, forming a single layer.
7. Spread the sautéed vegetable mixture evenly over the sweet potatoes.
8. Evenly distribute the egg mixture over the vegetables in the skillet.
9. If using, sprinkle the grated dairy-free cheese on top of the frittata.
10. Move the skillet to the preheated oven and bake it for 15-20 minutes until the frittata is firm and the top is slightly golden.
11. Once ready, remove it from the oven and let it cool slightly before slicing.
12. Garnish with chopped fresh parsley for color and flavor.
13. Serve the Savory Spinach and Sweet Potato Frittata warm, and savor every bite of this nutritious morning delight.

RECIPE TIP: Customize this frittata by adding your favorite veggies or herbs, such as diced tomatoes, sliced mushrooms, or fresh basil.

SUBSTITUTION TIP: To make the frittata vegan, substitute the eggs with a tofu-based egg alternative and use plant-based milk.

NUTRITIONAL INFORMATION PER SERVING: Calories: 215; Total Fat: 14g; Total Cholesterol: 186g; Sugar: 3g; Fiber: 3.5g; Protein: 11g; Sodium: 200mg; Potassium: 470mg

Begin your day with a tasty and wholesome treat by trying our Blueberry Almond Flour Delight Pancakes. These light and fluffy pancakes are gluten-free and filled with juicy blueberries and a good amount of protein and healthy fats to keep you going.

BLUEBERRY ALMOND FLOUR DELIGHT PANCAKES

✅ Servings: 2
(4 pancakes each)

✅ Preparation time: 10 min

✅ Cooking time: 15 min

- 1 cup almond flour
- 1/2 teaspoon baking powder
- Pinch of salt
- 2 large eggs
- 1/4 cup of any unsweetened plant-based milk (consider almond)

- 1 tablespoon maple syrup (optional)
- 1/4 teaspoon cinnamon
- 1 teaspoon vanilla extract
- 1/2 cup fresh blueberries
- Coconut oil or cooking spray for greasing

1. Blend a pinch of salt, baking powder, almond flour, and cinnamon in a mixing bowl.
2. Use another bowl to whisk together the eggs, almond milk, maple syrup (if using), and vanilla extract until well combined.
3. Mix the wet and dry components thoroughly to achieve a uniform consistency of the batter.
4. Gently fold in the fresh blueberries.
5. Heat a non-stick skillet or griddle over medium heat. Use a light coat of coconut oil or cooking spray on the surface.
6. Pour a small amount of batter onto the skillet to form pancakes (about 1/4 cup for each pancake).
7. Cook the pancakes on one side for 2-3 minutes until bubbles form on the surface. Flip and cook for 2-3 minutes on the other side, until golden brown and cooked through.
8. Repeat the same procedure with the batter left, greasing the skillet as needed.
9. Once cooked, transfer the pancakes to serving plates.
10. Serve the Blueberry Almond Flour Delight Pancakes warm, topped with additional fresh blueberries, a teaspoon of yogurt, or a drizzle of maple syrup, if desired.

RECIPE TIP: For an added crunch and flavor, consider mixing in a handful of chopped almonds or walnuts to the batter before cooking.

SUBSTITUTION TIP:
- Get creative with toppings! Try sliced bananas, chopped nuts, or a sprinkle of cinnamon for added flavor and texture.
- If you prefer to avoid added sugars, omit the maple syrup and rely on the natural sweetness of the blueberries.

NUTRITIONAL INFORMATION PER SERVING: Calories: 320; Total Fat: 24g; Total Cholesterol: 185g; Sugar: 6g; Fiber: 6g; Protein: 13g; Sodium: 190mg; Potassium: 300mg

Warm up your morning routine with the heartwarming and nourishing delight of Apple Cinnamon Comfort Quinoa Porridge. This dish is a wholesome and comforting choice and a step towards reducing inflammation and promoting overall well-being.

APPLE CINNAMON QUINOA PORRIDGE

✅ Servings: 2　　　✅ Preparation time: 10 min　　　✅ Cooking time: 10 min

- 1/2 cup quinoa, rinsed and drained
- 1 cup any unsweetened plant-based milk of choice (consider almond)
- 1 cup water
- 1 apple, peeled, cored, and chopped
- 1/2 teaspoon ground cinnamon
- 1/4 teaspoon ground nutmeg
- Pinch of salt
- 1 tablespoon pure maple syrup (for sweetness, optional)
- Chopped walnuts for topping
- Fresh berries for topping

1. Mix the rinsed quinoa almond milk, water, chopped apple, ground cinnamon, ground nutmeg, and a pinch of salt in a medium saucepan.
2. Heat the mixture on medium heat until it boils. Once boiling, place it in a covered saucepan on low heat and let it simmer for 15-20 minutes until it has fully cooked and absorbed the liquid. Stir occasionally to prevent sticking.
3. If using, stir in the pure maple syrup to add sweetness to the porridge.
4. Take the saucepan off the stove and cover it. Set it aside for 5 minutes so that the flavors can mix.
5. Give the porridge a good stir to fluff up the quinoa and distribute the apple pieces evenly.
6. Serve the porridge in bowls, topped with chopped walnuts and fresh berries for added texture and antioxidants.

RECIPE TIP: Customize your porridge by adding a sprinkle of ground flaxseeds or chia seeds to boost omega-3 fatty acids and fiber.

SUBSTITUTION TIP:
- You can use honey or coconut sugar instead of maple syrup for sweetness.
- Experiment with fruits like pears, berries, or peaches for a varied flavor profile.
- If you have nut allergies, use oat or any other nut-free plant-based milk and top your porridge with toasted pumpkin or sunflower seeds to avoid nuts.

NUTRITIONAL INFORMATION PER SERVING: Calories: 255; Total Fat: 5g; Total Cholesterol: 0mg; Sugar: 11g; Fiber: 7g; Protein: 5g; Sodium: 56mg; Potassium: 318mg

Start your day with the delicious and nutritious Banana Walnut Creamy Smoothie. This smoothie is loaded with anti-inflammatory ingredients that taste delicious and help enhance your overall wellness.

BANANA WALNUT CREAMY SMOOTHIE

 Servings: 2   Preparation time: 5 min   Cooking time: 0 min

- 2 ripe bananas, peeled and sliced
- 1/4 cup walnuts
- 1 cup of any plant-based milk (consider almond)
- 1 tablespoon chia seeds
- 1/2 teaspoon ground cinnamon
- 1/2 teaspoon pure vanilla extract
- Ice cubes (optional)

1. Combine the sliced bananas, walnuts, almond milk, ground cinnamon, chia seeds, and pure vanilla extract in a blender.
2. Add a handful of ice cubes for a colder and more refreshing smoothie (optional).
3. Blend the ingredients at high speed until the mixture becomes smooth and creamy, typically taking 1-2 minutes.
4. Stop the blender and scrape down the sides if needed, then blend again for a few seconds to ensure all ingredients are well incorporated.
5. Pour the creamy smoothie into glasses and serve immediately.

RECIPE TIP: To enhance the nutritional profile of your smoothie, consider adding a tablespoon of flaxseeds for extra omega-3 fatty acids and fiber.

SUBSTITUTION TIP:
- Nut-Free Version: If you have nut allergies, replace the walnuts with sunflower or pumpkin seeds for a nut-free alternative.
- Sweetener Addition: If you prefer a sweeter smoothie, add honey or a drizzle of pure maple syrup to taste.
- Milk Alternatives: Use any unsweetened plant-based milk that suits your taste, such as oat or coconut.
- Creamier Texture: Add half an avocado to the blender and other ingredients for an even creamier texture.
- Extra Flavor Boost: Enhance the flavor with a dash of nutmeg or a pinch of ground ginger for a subtle spicy kick.

NUTRITIONAL INFORMATION PER SERVING: Calories: 250; Total Fat: 14g; Total cholesterol: 0mg; Sugar: 17g; Fiber: 6g; Protein: 5g; Sodium: 87mg; Potassium: 493mg

Enjoy these delicious and nourishing Fluffy Buckwheat Banana Pancakes as a wholesome way to start your morning and kickstart your wellness journey with an anti-inflammatory diet.

These pancakes are made with nutritious ingredients and natural sweeteners, creating a delicious combination of taste and health benefits.

FLUFFY BUCKWHEAT BANANA PANCAKES

✔ Servings: 2   ✔ Preparation time: 10 min   ✔ Cooking time: 15 min

- 1 cup buckwheat flour
- 1 ripe banana, mashed
- 1 teaspoon baking powder
- 1/4 teaspoon salt
- 1/2 teaspoon ground cinnamon

- 1 cup of any non-dairy milk (consider almond)
- 1 tablespoon maple syrup (optional)
- 1 teaspoon vanilla extract
- Coconut oil for cooking

1. Combine the buckwheat flour, salt, baking powder, and ground cinnamon in a large mixing bowl.
2. Mash the ripe banana in another bowl until smooth. Add the almond milk, maple syrup (if using), and vanilla extract. Mix well until the wet ingredients are thoroughly combined.
3. Pour the wet ingredients into the dry ingredients. Stir gently until just combined. It's okay if there are a few lumps in the batter.
4. Preheat a non-stick skillet or griddle on medium heat. Lightly grease the surface with a small amount of coconut oil.
5. Once the skillet is hot, pour a quarter cup of the pancake batter onto the skillet for each pancake. Cook until tiny bubbles form on the surface, about 2-3 minutes.
6. Carefully flip the pancakes and cook on the other side for 2-3 minutes until they are golden brown and cooked through.
7. Remove the pancakes from the skillet and keep warm. Repeat the process with the remaining batter.

RECIPE TIP: For extra flavor, add a handful of chopped nuts or fresh berries to the pancake batter before cooking.

SUBSTITUTION TIP:
- To make the pancakes vegan, use the non-dairy milk of your choice and omit the maple syrup (or replace it with a vegan-friendly sweetener).
- If you don't have buckwheat flour, use a gluten-free or whole-wheat flour blend.
- Feel free to customize the pancakes with your favorite toppings, such as sliced bananas, berries, chopped nuts, or a drizzle of nut butter.

NUTRITIONAL INFORMATION PER SERVING: Calories: 280; Total Fat: 3g; Total Cholesterol: 0g; Sugar: 8g; Fiber: 6g; Protein: 8g; Sodium: 240mg; Potassium: 340mg

Enjoy the refreshing and nourishing Mango Turmeric Morning Lassi as a delightful way to embrace an anti-inflammatory diet and infuse your morning with health-boosting ingredients.

This lassi, packed with the vibrant sweetness of mangoes and the health-boosting properties of turmeric, is a refreshing and nutritious way to kickstart your morning.

MANGO TURMERIC MORNING LASSI

✓ Servings: 2   ✓ Preparation time: 5 min   ✓ Cooking time: 0 min

- 1 ripe mango, peeled and diced
- 1 cup plain yogurt (Greek yogurt or dairy-free alternative)
- 1/2 teaspoon ground turmeric
- 1/2 teaspoon ground ginger
- 1 teaspoon honey (optional)
- A pinch of black pepper
- Ice cubes

1. Combine the diced mango, plain yogurt, ground turmeric, ginger, honey (if using), and a pinch of black pepper in a blender.
2. Mix the ingredients in a blender on high speed until smooth and creamy. If the lassi is too thick, add a splash of water or more yogurt to achieve your desired consistency.
3. To achieve your desired level of sweetness, you can add more honey as necessary and adjust to taste. Blend again to incorporate.
4. Add several ice cubes to the blender and blend briefly to chill and slightly froth the lassi.
5. Pour the Mango Turmeric Morning Lassi into glasses and serve immediately.

RECIPE TIP: A pinch of black pepper is recommended to enhance the absorption of turmeric's beneficial compounds. The black pepper contains piperine, which can improve curcumin's bioavailability, the active turmeric compound.

SUBSTITUTION TIP:
- For a dairy-free version, use coconut yogurt or almond milk yogurt.
- If fresh mango is unavailable, you can use frozen mango chunks. Make sure to thaw them slightly before blending.
- Customize the sweetness by adjusting the amount of honey or using alternative sweeteners like maple syrup or agave nectar.

NUTRITIONAL INFORMATION PER SERVING: Calories: 150; Total Fat: 2g; Total Cholesterol: 8mg; Sugar: 22g; Fiber: 2g; Protein: 6g; Sodium: 60mg; Potassium: 330mg

Experience the lively and pleasant taste of a mix of berries and the satisfying crunch of almond granola in this delightful Mixed Berry Parfait. This energizing breakfast option is a feast for the taste buds and a nourishing way to kickstart your day with anti-inflammatory goodness.

MIXED BERRY PARFAIT WITH CRUNCHY ALMOND GRANOLA

 Servings: 2   Preparation time: 10 min   ✅ Cooking time: 0 min

For the Crunchy Almond Granola:
- 1 cup rolled oats
- 1/2 cup chopped almonds
- 2 tablespoons honey or maple syrup
- 1 tablespoon extra-virgin olive oil
- 1/2 teaspoon ground cinnamon
- Pinch of salt

Crunchy Almond Granola:
1. Preheat oven to 325°F (165°C) and line a parchment paper on a baking pan.
2. Combine rolled oats, chopped almonds, honey or maple syrup, extra-virgin olive oil, and ground cinnamon in a bowl and a pinch of salt. Mix well until the oats and almonds are coated with the sweet mixture.
3. Evenly spread the mixture onto the prepared baking sheet.
4. Place in the preheated oven and bake for 15-20 minutes or until the granola turns golden brown and crisp. To achieve even toasting, stir the granola once or twice while baking.
5. Remove from the oven and let the granola cool completely on the baking sheet. Once cooled, break it into clusters.

For the Mixed Berry Parfait:
- 1 cup of mixed berries (raspberries, blueberries, strawberries, etc.)
- 1 cup plain yogurt (Greek yogurt or dairy-free alternative)
- 2 tablespoons chia seeds

Mixed Berry Parfait:
1. Wash and prepare the mixed berries as needed. You can slice strawberries if desired.
2. Start by layering a spoonful of yogurt at the bottom in serving glasses or bowls.
3. Add a layer of mixed berries on top of the yogurt.
4. Sprinkle a layer of chia seeds over the berries.
5. Add a layer of the Crunchy Almond Granola.
6. Repeat the layering process with yogurt, berries, chia seeds, and granola until the glasses are filled.
7. Finish with a final sprinkle of granola on top for added crunch and visual appeal.

RECIPE TIP: Make a larger batch of Crunchy Almond Granola and store it in an airtight container for future use. It's a versatile topping for various dishes, including yogurt, smoothie bowls, and oatmeal.

SUBSTITUTION TIP: Customize the yogurt using your preferred type, such as Greek yogurt or a dairy-free alternative like coconut yogurt or almond yogurt.

NUTRITIONAL INFORMATION PER SERVING: Calories: 350; Total Fat: 15g; Total Cholesterol: 5mg; Sugar: 20g; Fiber: 8g; Protein: 12g; Sodium: 50mg; Potassium: 350mg

Start your day with a burst of energy and nutrients from our Green Goddess Breakfast Bowl. Creamy avocado pairs perfectly with a vibrant medley of greens and seeds to create a satisfying and nourishing breakfast.

GREEN GODDESS BREAKFAST BOWL WITH CREAMY AVOCADO

✔ Servings: 2   ✔ Preparation time: 15 min   ✔ Cooking time: 0 min

- 2 ripe avocados
- 2 cups baby spinach leaves
- 1 cup kale, stems removed and chopped
- 1/2 cucumber, sliced
- 1/2 cup broccoli florets
- 2 tablespoons pumpkin seeds

- 2 tablespoons sunflower seeds
- 2 tablespoons chia seeds
- 1 tablespoon extra-virgin olive oil
- Juice of 1 lemon
- Salt and pepper to taste

1. To prepare the avocados, cut them in half and remove the pits. Then, scoop out the flesh and place it in a bowl.
2. Mash the avocado until it becomes smooth and creamy in texture using a fork.
3. Combine the baby spinach, chopped kale, cucumber slices, and broccoli florets in a separate bowl.
4. Drizzle the greens with extra-virgin olive oil and the juice of one lemon. Add a pinch of salt and pepper. Toss to coat the greens evenly.
5. To assemble the breakfast bowl, divide the mashed avocado between two bowls, spreading it at the bottom.
6. Top the avocado with the mixed greens, arranging them in a mound in the center.
7. Sprinkle pumpkin, sunflower, and chia seeds over the greens to add crunch and nutritional value.

RECIPE TIP: Customize your Green Goddess Breakfast Bowl by adding a poached egg or a sprinkle of crumbled feta cheese on the top for extra protein and flavor.

SUBSTITUTION TIP:
- Nut-Free Variation: If you're allergic to nuts, you can omit the pumpkin seeds and substitute them with hemp seeds or shredded coconut for added texture.
- Lemon Alternatives: If you prefer a different tangy flavor, you can use lime juice instead of lemon juice.
- Greens Substitutions: Feel free to switch out the baby spinach and kale for other leafy greens like arugula, Swiss chard, or collard greens.
- Herb Infusion: Add fresh herbs like mint, basil, or parsley to the greens for an aromatic twist.

NUTRITIONAL INFORMATION PER SERVING: Calories: 360; Total Fat: 29g; Total Cholesterol: 0mg; Sugar: 4g; Fiber: 14g; Protein: 10g; Sodium: 75mg; Potassium: 1370mg

Enjoy a delightful, anti-inflammatory morning treat with creamy avocado, crisp radishes, and fresh micro greens.

AVOCADO DREAM TOAST WITH RADISH AND MICROGREENS

 Servings: 2   Preparation time: 10 min   Cooking time: 0 min

- 2 slices whole wheat bread (gluten-free if needed)
- 1 ripe avocado
- 4-6 radishes, thinly sliced
- Salt and pepper to taste

- 1/2 cup microgreens (such as broccoli or sunflower sprouts)
- 1 tablespoon extra-virgin olive oil
- 1 teaspoon lemon juice

1. Toast the slices of whole wheat bread until they are crispy and golden brown.
2. Cut the ripe avocado in half while the bread is toasting, and remove the pit. Scoop the pulp into a bowl and use a fork to mash it until it becomes a smooth consistency.
3. Drizzle the mashed avocado with lemon juice and extra-virgin olive oil and season with a dash of pepper and a pinch of salt. Mix well to combine.
4. Once the bread is toasted, spread a generous layer of the mashed avocado mixture onto each slice.
5. Arrange the thinly sliced radishes over the avocado spread.
6. Sprinkle the microgreens over the radishes, adding fresh flavor and nutrients.
7. Finish by drizzling more extra-virgin olive oil over the toast and garnish with an additional sprinkle of salt and pepper if desired.

RECIPE TIP: Add a poached egg or a sprinkle of crumbled feta cheese to make this dish even more filling.

SUBSTITUTION TIP:
- Radish Substitutions: If radishes are not your preference, you can substitute them with thinly sliced cucumbers or colorful bell peppers.
- Microgreens Variation: Feel free to experiment with different microgreens, such as pea shoots or watercress, for various flavors and nutrients.
- Gluten-Free Option: Use gluten-free bread to make this recipe suitable for those with gluten sensitivities.

NUTRITIONAL INFORMATION PER SERVING: Calories: 230; Total Fat: 16g; Total Cholesterol: 0mg; Sugar: 2g; Fiber: 6g; Protein: 4g; Sodium: 150mg; Potassium: 480mg

This omelet is a delicious and healthy way to begin your day with anti-inflammatory properties. It is filled with sautéed spinach and mushrooms, making it a hearty and satisfying meal.

SAVORY SPINACH AND MUSHROOM OMELETTE

✓ Servings: 1   ✓ Preparation time: 10 min   ✓ Cooking time: 10 min

- 2 large eggs
- 1/4 cup chopped spinach
- 1/4 cup sliced mushrooms
- 1/4 cup diced bell peppers (any color)
- 1/4 cup diced tomatoes
- 1 tablespoon extra-virgin olive oil
- Salt and pepper, to taste
- Pinch of turmeric (optional)
- Fresh herbs for garnish, such as parsley or chives

1. Crack the eggs in a bowl and whisk them until well combined. Add a pinch of salt and pepper. Place aside.
2. Heat the extra-virgin olive oil in a non-stick skillet over medium heat.
3. Add the sliced mushrooms and sauté for 2-3 minutes until brown.
4. Add the chopped spinach and diced bell peppers to the skillet. Sauté for an additional 2 minutes until the vegetables are slightly wilted.
5. Pour the whisked eggs over the sautéed vegetables in the skillet. Allow the eggs to cook undisturbed for a minute or two until the edges start to set.
6. Gently raise the sides of the omelet using a spatula and then tilt the pan to let the raw egg flow towards the edges.
7. Sprinkle the diced tomatoes over one-half of the omelet. Optionally, add a pinch of turmeric for its anti-inflammatory benefits.
8. Carefully fold the other half of the omelet over the tomatoes to create a half-moon shape. Press down gently with the spatula to ensure the omelet is cooked through.
9. Continue cooking for another 2-3 minutes until the omelet is cooked to your desired level of doneness.
10. Slide the omelet onto a plate, garnish with fresh herbs, and serve hot.

RECIPE TIP: You can customize your omelet by adding other anti-inflammatory ingredients such as diced avocado, sautéed onions, or a sprinkle of nutritional yeast for a cheesy flavor.

SUBSTITUTION TIP:
- For a dairy-free option, you can use a plant-based alternative to eggs, such as tofu scramble, chickpea flour batter, or a combination of chickpea flour and water.
- You can exclude the turmeric or incorporate a small quantity if you want a less intense taste.

NUTRITIONAL INFORMATION PER SERVING: Calories: 250; Total Fat: 18g; Total Cholesterol: 370mg; Sugar: 3g; Fiber: 4g; Protein: 15g; Sodium: 270mg; Potassium: 450mg

Begin your day with vitality and nourishment through these delightful Rise-and-Shine Overnight Oats. A blend of wholesome oats, vibrant berries, and nutrient-rich seeds, this breakfast is a breeze to prepare and ensures sustained energy throughout your morning.

PEACHY GINGER SUNRISE SMOOTHIE

✅ Servings: 1   ✅ Preparation time: 5 min   ✅ Cooking time: 0 min

- 1 ripe peach, pitted and chopped
- 1/2 banana, sliced
- 1/2 cup unsweetened non-dairy milk (consider almond)
- 1/2 teaspoon freshly grated ginger
- 1/2 teaspoon ground turmeric
- 1 teaspoon chia seeds
- 1/4 teaspoon pure vanilla extract
- Ice cubes, as needed

1. Combine the chopped peach, sliced banana, almond milk, grated ginger, ground turmeric, chia seeds, and pure vanilla extract in a blender.
2. Add several ice cubes to the blender to make the smoothie cold and refreshing.
3. Blend on high until all the ingredients are well combined and the smoothie is smooth and creamy. If the mixture is too thick, add some more almond milk.
4. Taste the smoothie and adjust the sweetness if needed. Add a drizzle of honey or a Medjool date for extra sweetness if desired.
5. Once the smoothie reaches your desired consistency and flavor, pour it into a glass.
6. Garnish with a slice of peach or a sprinkle of chia seeds for an additional visual and textural element.
7. Enjoy your Peachy Ginger Sunrise Smoothie immediately to savor its freshness and anti-inflammatory benefits.

RECIPE TIP: Add a scoop of plant-based protein powder to the smoothie for added creaminess and a protein boost. Make sure to choose a protein powder that aligns with the anti-inflammatory principles of the diet.

SUBSTITUTION TIP:
- If you're not a fan of peaches, you can substitute with mango or nectarines for a similar tropical flavor profile.
- Swap the almond milk with coconut or oat milk if you prefer a different non-dairy milk.
- Fresh turmeric root can be used instead of ground turmeric for an even more potent anti-inflammatory kick.

NUTRITIONAL INFORMATION PER SERVING: Calories: 160; Total Fat: 3g; Total Cholesterol: 0mg; Sugar: 17g; Fiber: 6g; Protein: 2g; Sodium: 85mg; Potassium: 450mg

Start your day on a vibrant and refreshing note with this Peachy Ginger Sunrise Smoothie. This smoothie is infused with the delicious flavor of juicy peaches and the refreshing kick of ginger, making it a fantastic choice for those looking to increase their energy levels and alleviate inflammation.

SPICED PUMPKIN MORNING COOKIES

✅ Servings: 12 cookies   ✅ Preparation time: 15 min   ✅ Cooking time: 15 min

- 1 cup rolled oats
- 1 cup whole wheat flour
- 1 teaspoon ground cinnamon
- 1/2 teaspoon ground nutmeg
- 1/2 teaspoon ground ginger
- 1/4 teaspoon ground cloves
- 1/2 teaspoon baking powder
- 1/4 teaspoon baking soda
- 1/4 teaspoon salt

- 1/2 cup pure pumpkin puree
- 1/4 cup pure maple syrup
- 1/4 cup unsweetened applesauce
- 1/4 cup sesame seeds
- 1/4 cup pecans or chopped walnuts (optional)
- 1/4 cup dried raisins or cranberries (optional)

1. Preheat the oven to 350°F (175°C) and place a sheet of parchment paper onto a baking tray.
2. Combine the rolled oats, whole wheat flour, ground cinnamon, ground nutmeg, ginger, salt, baking soda, baking powder, and cloves in a large mixing bowl.
3. Mix the pumpkin puree, maple syrup, and unsweetened applesauce in another bowl until well combined.
4. Add the wet and dry ingredients and stir until a thick cookie dough forms.
5. Add sesame seeds, and if desired, fold in the chopped walnuts or pecans and dried raisins or cranberries for added texture and flavor.
6. Use a cookie scoop or spoon to scoop spoonfuls of the cookie dough onto the ready baking tray, spacing them about 2 inches apart.
7. Gently flatten each cookie with the back of the spoon to create a cookie shape.
8. Move the tray into the preheated oven and bake until the cookies take on a golden brown hue at the edges (approximately 12 to 15 minutes).
9. Remove the baking sheet from the oven and let the cookies cool for a few minutes before moving them to a wire rack for complete cooling.

RECIPE TIP: These cookies are not overly sweet, making them a tremendous guilt-free breakfast option. Pour a drizzle of maple syrup into the cookie dough if you prefer a sweeter taste.

SUBSTITUTION TIP: If you're not a fan of pumpkin, you can substitute it with mashed sweet potato for a similar texture and natural sweetness.

NUTRITIONAL INFORMATION PER COOKIE: Calories: 110; Total Fat: 2g; Total Cholesterol: 0mg; Sugar: 6g; Fiber: 3g; Protein: 3g; Sodium: 95mg; Potassium: 85mg

WHOLESOME
Lunches

Indulge in the flavors of the Mediterranean with this vibrant and nutrient-packed Anti-Inflammatory Salad. This salad is packed with vibrant veggies, nutritious grains, and nourishing fats. It's a tasty way to promote good health and reduce inflammation.

MEDITERRANEAN MAGIC ANTI-INFLAMMATORY SALAD

 Servings: 4   Preparation time: 20 min   Cooking time: 0 min

For the Salad:

- 2 cups mixed greens (spinach, kale, arugula)
- 1 cup cherry tomatoes, halved
- 1 cucumber, diced
- 1/2 red bell pepper, diced
- 1/4 red onion, thinly sliced
- 1/2 cup cooked quinoa
- 1/4 cup Kalamata olives, halved and pitted
- 2 tablespoons chopped fresh parsley
- 2 tablespoons chopped fresh basil
- 1/4 cup crumbled feta cheese (optional)

For the Dressing:

- 3 tablespoons extra-virgin olive oil
- 1 tablespoon red wine vinegar
- 1 clove garlic, minced
- 1 teaspoon dried oregano
- Salt and ground black pepper to taste

1. Combine the mixed greens, cherry tomatoes, red onion, cucumber, and red bell pepper in a large salad bowl.
2. Add the cooked quinoa to the salad and gently toss to combine.
3. Sprinkle the Kalamata olives, crumbled feta cheese (if using), chopped parsley, and chopped basil over the salad.
4. Combine the minced garlic, extra-virgin olive oil, red wine vinegar, dried oregano, black pepper, and salt to create the dressing.
5. Pour the dressing onto the salad and toss everything together until the ingredients are well-coated.
6. Serve the Mediterranean Magic Anti-Inflammatory Salad in individual plates or bowls.

RECIPE TIP: For an extra boost of protein, you can add grilled chicken, chickpeas, or roasted turkey breast to the salad.

SUBSTITUTION TIP:
- Exclude the feta cheese or substitute it with crumbled tofu seasoned with a pinch of nutritional yeast to make this salad vegan.
- If you're not a fan of quinoa, you can use cooked brown rice, farro, or barley as an alternative whole grain.

NUTRITIONAL INFORMATION PER SERVING: Calories: 230; Total Fat: 16g; Total Cholesterol: 10mg; Sugar: 4g; Fiber: 4g; Protein: 6g; Sodium: 220mg; Potassium: 320mg

Elevate your lunchtime with this satisfying and flavorful wrap. Grilled chicken, creamy avocado, and a burst of fresh herbs are beautifully wrapped in a whole wheat tortilla, creating a delightful and nutritious meal perfect for your anti-inflammatory diet.

GRILLED CHICKEN AND AVOCADO DELIGHT WRAP WITH HERB INFUSION

✔ Servings: 2   ✔ Preparation time: 15 min   ✔ Cooking time: 10 min

- 2 boneless, skinless chicken breasts
- 1 tablespoon extra-virgin olive oil
- 1 teaspoon dried oregano
- Ground black pepper and salt to taste
- 2 whole wheat tortillas
- 1 ripe avocado, sliced
- 1 cup mixed salad greens (arugula, spinach, etc.)
- 1/4 cup chopped fresh cilantro
- 1/4 cup chopped fresh parsley
- Juice of 1 lime
- 1 teaspoon minced garlic

1. Preheat the grill or stovetop grill pan over medium-high heat.
2. Mix the extra-virgin olive oil, dried oregano, salt, and black pepper in a small bowl. Brush the chicken breasts with this mixture.
3. Grill the chicken breasts for about 4-5 minutes per side or until they are cooked and have excellent grill marks. Ensure the internal temperature reaches 165°F (74°C). Once done, set aside to rest for a few minutes.
4. While the chicken rests, warm the whole wheat tortillas on the grill or stovetop for about 15-20 seconds on each side.
5. Combine the chopped cilantro, chopped parsley, lime juice, and minced garlic in a separate bowl to create an herb infusion.
6. Slice the grilled chicken breasts into thin strips.
7. Place a whole wheat tortilla on a clean surface to assemble the wraps. Layer sliced avocado, mixed salad greens, and sliced grilled chicken on one side of the tortilla. Drizzle the herb infusion over the filling.
8. Carefully fold the tortilla over the filling and roll it up tightly to form a wrap.

RECIPE TIP: For added crunch and texture, consider adding thinly sliced red bell pepper or cucumber to the wrap.

SUBSTITUTION TIP:
- To make this wrap vegetarian, substitute grilled tofu or tempeh for the chicken.
- If you prefer a dairy-free option, omit the lime-infused herbs and add balsamic vinegar or a dollop of hummus for extra flavor.
- Customize the wrap by adding other anti-inflammatory vegetables like tomatoes, shredded carrots, sliced radishes, or baby spinach.

NUTRITIONAL INFORMATION PER SERVING: Calories: 420; Total Fat: 22g; Total Cholesterol: 70mg; Sugar: 2g; Fiber: 7g; Protein: 35g; Sodium: 320mg; Potassium: 880mg

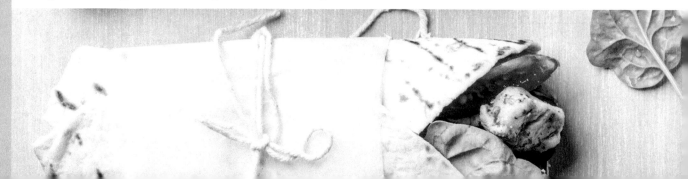

Indulge in the comforting flavors of this Lentil Sunshine Soup with the warming touch of turmeric. It's a delightful and wholesome choice for lunch, embodying the principles of an anti-inflammatory diet.

LENTIL SUNSHINE SOUP WITH A TOUCH OF TURMERIC

 Servings: 6   Preparation time: 15 min   Cooking time: 30 min

- 1 cup dried green lentils, drained and rinsed
- 1 medium sweet potato, peeled and diced
- 2 medium carrots, peeled and diced
- 1 yellow onion, chopped
- 2 cloves garlic, minced
- 1 teaspoon ground turmeric
- 1/2 teaspoon ground cumin
- 1/4 teaspoon ground ginger
- 6 cups vegetable broth
- 1 cup diced tomatoes (canned or fresh)
- 2 cups baby spinach leaves
- 1 tablespoon extra-virgin olive oil
- Ground black pepper and salt to taste

1. Warm the olive oil on medium heat in a sizable pot. Add the chopped onion and cook until it turns translucent, about 3-4 minutes.
2. Mix minced garlic, turmeric, ground cumin, and ginger. Continue to cook for an additional 1 to 2 minutes until a delightful fragrance fills the air.
3. Add the diced sweet potato and carrots to the pot. Mix thoroughly and ensure the vegetables are fully coated with the spices.
4. Add the vegetable broth and the diced tomatoes to the mixture. Heat your mixture until it reaches boiling point, reduce the heat to low, and then cover the pot. Let the soup simmer for about 20-25 minutes or until the lentils and vegetables are tender.
5. Add the baby spinach leaves to the pot and stir until wilted.
6. Season the soup with salt and freshly ground black pepper to taste.
7. Serve the Lentil Sunshine Soup warm, garnished, and adorned with a light scattering of freshly chopped cilantro or parsley, if desired.

RECIPE TIP: For added creaminess, blend a portion of the soup using an immersion blender before adding the spinach. This will give the soup a rich and silky texture.

SUBSTITUTION TIP:
- Swap green lentils with red lentils if desired. Red lentils tend to cook faster and become softer, creating a different texture for the soup.
- Customize the vegetables by adding zucchini, bell peppers, or celery for extra variety and nutrition.

NUTRITIONAL INFORMATION PER SERVING: Calories: 214; Total Fat: 3g; Total Cholesterol: 0mg; Sugar: 6g; Fiber: 12g; Protein: 12g; Sodium: 561mg; Potassium: 799mg

Enjoy the refreshing flavors of this Spinach and Strawberry Bliss Salad, a delightful medley of nutrient-rich spinach, juicy strawberries, and a symphony of balsamic dressing. This salad perfectly balances sweetness and tanginess, making it a true treat for your taste buds.

SPINACH AND STRAWBERRY BLISS SALAD WITH BALSAMIC SYMPHONY

 Servings: 4   Preparation time: 15 min   Cooking time: 0 min

- 6 cups fresh spinach leaves, washed and dried
- 2 cups fresh strawberries, sliced
- 1/2 cup red onion, thinly sliced
- 1/2 cup chopped walnuts

- 1/4 cup crumbled feta cheese
- 2 tablespoons extra-virgin olive oil
- 2 tablespoons balsamic vinegar
- 1 teaspoon honey
- Salt and ground black pepper to taste

1. Combine the fresh spinach leaves, sliced strawberries, thinly sliced red onion, and chopped walnuts in a large salad bowl.
2. Mix the extra-virgin olive oil, balsamic vinegar, honey, salt, and ground black pepper in a small bowl to create the dressing.
3. Drizzle the dressing over the salad ingredients in a large bowl.
4. Gently toss all the ingredients together to ensure an even distribution of the dressing.
5. Sprinkle the crumbled feta cheese over the top of the salad.
6. Serve the Spinach and Strawberry Bliss Salad immediately, allowing guests to enjoy the combination of flavors and textures.

RECIPE TIP: To enhance the nutty flavor and add a crunch, toast the chopped walnuts in a dry skillet over medium heat until fragrant. Let the walnuts cool before adding them to the salad.

SUBSTITUTION TIP:
- Replace fresh strawberries with raspberries or blueberries for a different berry twist.
- For a vegan version, exclude the feta cheese or use a dairy-free alternative.
- Swap the honey in the dressing with maple syrup or agave nectar for a vegan-friendly option.

NUTRITIONAL INFORMATION PER SERVING: Calories: 220; Total Fat: 15g; Total Cholesterol: 5mg; Sugar: 9g; Fiber: 4g; Protein: 4g; Sodium: 125mg; Potassium: 375mg

Enjoy the wonderful blend of textures and flavors in this Roasted Vegetable and Quinoa Symphony Salad. Nutrient-packed quinoa, vibrant roasted vegetables, and a zesty vinaigrette come together to create a satisfying lunch that's as delicious as it is nutritious.

ROASTED VEGETABLE AND QUINOA SYMPHONY SALAD

 Servings: 4   Preparation time: 15 min   Cooking time: 25 min

For the Salad:
- 1 cup quinoa, rinsed and drained
- 2 cups mixed vegetables (bell peppers, zucchini, cherry tomatoes), chopped
- 1 red onion, thinly sliced
- 2 tablespoons extra-virgin olive oil
- Salt and ground black pepper to taste

For the Vinaigrette Dressing:
- 3 tablespoons balsamic vinegar
- 2 tablespoons extra-virgin olive oil
- 1 teaspoon Dijon mustard
- 1 teaspoon honey (optional)
- Salt and ground black pepper to taste

1. Preheat the oven to 400°F (200°C).
2. Combine the rinsed quinoa with 2 cups of water in a medium saucepan. Bring to a boil, then reduce the heat to low, cover, and simmer for about 15 minutes until the quinoa is cooked and the water is absorbed. Fluff the quinoa with a fork and put it aside.
3. Toss the mixed vegetables and red onion with the extra-virgin olive oil, salt, and freshly ground black pepper on a baking sheet.
4. Roast the vegetables in the preheated oven for about 20-25 minutes or until they are tender and slightly caramelized.
5. Whisk together the balsamic vinegar, extra-virgin olive oil, Dijon mustard, salt, ground black pepper, and honey (if using) in a small bowl to create the vinaigrette.
6. Combine the cooked quinoa and roasted vegetables in a large salad bowl. Drizzle the vinaigrette over the mixture and gently toss to coat all the ingredients.
7. Serve the Roasted Vegetable and Quinoa Symphony Salad warm or at room temperature, allowing the flavors to shine.

RECIPE TIP: Customize this salad by adding your favorite anti-inflammatory herbs, such as fresh basil or oregano, for an extra burst of flavor.

SUBSTITUTION TIP:
- Mix and match vegetables based on what's in season or readily available.
- Make the salad vegan by omitting the honey in the vinaigrette or using a plant-based sweetener.

NUTRITIONAL INFORMATION PER SERVING: Calories: 290; Total Fat: 13g; Total Cholesterol: 0mg; Sugar: 8g; Fiber: 7g; Protein: 8g; Sodium: 150mg; Potassium: 525mg

Embark on a journey to the Mediterranean with these delightful Stuffed Zucchini Sailboats. These sailboats are filled with wholesome ingredients and bursting with vibrant flavors, making them the perfect lunch option. They'll transport your taste buds to the sunny shores of the Mediterranean.

MEDITERRANEAN STUFFED ZUCCHINI SAILBOATS

 Servings: 4   Preparation time: 20 min   Cooking time: 25 min

For the Stuffed Zucchini:

- 2 large zucchinis, halved lengthwise and seeds scooped out
- 1 tablespoon olive oil
- 1 cup cooked quinoa
- 1 cup cut cherry tomatoes
- 1/2 cup cucumber, diced
- 1/4 cup crumbled feta cheese
- Salt and pepper, to taste
- 1/4 cup finely chopped red onion
- 1/4 cup pitted and chopped Kalamata olives
- 2 tablespoons chopped fresh parsley
- 2 tablespoons chopped fresh mint

For the Lemon-Herb Dressing:

- 2 tablespoons extra-virgin olive oil
- 2 tablespoons freshly squeezed lemon juice
- 1 clove garlic, minced
- 1 teaspoon dried oregano
- Salt and pepper, to taste

1. Preheat the oven to 375°F (190°C).
2. Place the zucchini halves on a baking sheet cut side up. Gently apply a light coating of extra-virgin olive oil onto them, season with salt and ground black pepper.
3. Bake the zucchini in the preheated oven for about 15 minutes or until they are slightly tender.
4. Combine the cooked quinoa, Kalamata olives, cherry tomatoes, red onion, cucumber, and crumbled feta cheese in a mixing bowl.
5. Whisk together the chopped parsley, fresh lemon juice, and extra-virgin olive oil in a small bowl to create the dressing.
6. Pour the dressing over the quinoa mixture and toss to combine.
7. Fill the zucchini halves generously with the quinoa mixture after baking them.
8. Place the stuffed zucchini sailboats back in the oven for 10 minutes, allowing the flavors to meld and the filling to warm.
9. Serve the Mediterranean Stuffed Zucchini Sailboats warm, garnished with additional chopped parsley if desired.

RECIPE TIP: Customize the filling by adding diced roasted red peppers or artichoke hearts for an extra burst of Mediterranean flavor.

SUBSTITUTION TIP:
- Make the dish vegan by omitting the feta cheese or using a dairy-free alternative.
- Swap quinoa for cooked brown rice or another whole grain of your choice.

NUTRITIONAL INFORMATION PER SERVING: Calories: 240; Total Fat: 14g; Total Cholesterol: 10mg; Sugar: 4g; Fiber: 5g; Protein: 6g; Sodium: 370mg; Potassium: 460mg

Enjoy the revitalizing flavors of the Crisp Cucumber Avocado Gazpacho. This vibrant and nutrient-rich soup is a fantastic light and anti-inflammatory lunch option, providing essential nutrients and hydration.

CRISP CUCUMBER AVOCADO GAZPACHO

✓ Servings: 4   ✓ Preparation time: 15 min   ✓ Cooking time: 0 min

- 2 large cucumbers, peeled, seeded, and chopped
- 1 ripe avocado, peeled and pitted
- 1 cup plain Greek yogurt
- 1/4 cup fresh cilantro leaves
- 1 small jalapeno with seeds removed and finely chopped

- 2 chopped green onions
- 2 tablespoons fresh lime juice
- 1/2 teaspoon ground cumin
- Salt and ground black pepper, to taste
- 1/4 cup water, as needed
- Fresh cilantro leaves for garnish

1. Combine the chopped cucumbers, ripe avocado, plain Greek yogurt, fresh cilantro leaves, chopped green onions, finely chopped jalapeno, fresh lime juice, and ground cumin in a food processor or blender.
2. Blend the ingredients on high speed until smooth and creamy, adding water as needed to achieve your desired consistency. The gazpacho should be slightly thick yet pourable.
3. Season the gazpacho with salt and freshly ground black pepper to taste. Blend again briefly to incorporate the seasoning.
4. Transfer the gazpacho to a bowl or individual serving glasses. Chill in the refrigerator for at least 30 min to allow the flavors to meld and the soup to become even more refreshing.
5. Before serving, garnish the gazpacho with fresh cilantro leaves for an added flavor.

RECIPE TIP: For an extra touch of freshness, serve the gazpacho with a drizzle of extra-virgin olive oil and a sprinkle of crushed red pepper flakes.

SUBSTITUTION TIP:
- To make the gazpacho dairy-free, use almond or coconut yogurt instead of Greek.
- Adjust the level of spiciness by adding more or less jalapeno, according to your preference.
- Substitute the jalapeno with a diced bell pepper for a milder flavor.

NUTRITIONAL INFORMATION PER SERVING: Calories: 160; Total Fat: 9g; Total Cholesterol: 5mg; Sugar: 6g; Fiber: 5g; Protein: 8g; Sodium: 80mg; Potassium: 660mg

Brown Rice Sushi Rolls are filled with the creamy goodness of avocado and the satisfying crunch of cucumber to enjoy every piece of sushi roll. This dish boasts a delightful blend of flavors and textures that will satisfy and energize you.

BROWN RICE SUSHI ROLLS WITH CREAMY AVOCADO AND CRUNCHY CUCUMBER

 Servings: 2   Preparation time: 20 min   ✅ Cooking time: 0 min

- 1 cup cooked brown rice, cooled down to room temperature
- 2 nori seaweed sheets
- 1 ripe avocado, thinly sliced
- 1/2 cucumber, julienned
- 2 tablespoons rice vinegar

- 1 teaspoon honey or maple syrup
- 1/2 teaspoon sea salt
- Soy sauce or tamari for dipping (optional)
- Pickled ginger and wasabi for serving (optional)

1. Mix the rice vinegar, sea salt, and honey or maple syrup in a small bowl until well combined. Drizzle this mixture over the cooked brown rice and gently toss to incorporate. Let the rice cool completely.
2. Place a bamboo sushi mat on a clean surface. Lay a nori seaweed sheet, shiny side down, on the mat.
3. Wet your fingers slightly to prevent the rice from sticking. Evenly spread half of the cooled brown rice over the nori, leaving a small border at the top.
4. Arrange avocado slices and julienned cucumber on the rice near the center.
5. Start rolling the nori from the bottom edge using the bamboo mat, applying gentle pressure to form a tight roll. Continue moving until you reach the top border. Dampen the top border slightly with water to seal the roll.
6. Repeat the process to make the second roll with the remaining ingredients.
7. Using a sharp knife, carefully slice each roll into bite-sized pieces. Wipe the blade with a damp cloth between every cut to prevent sticking.
8. If desired, serve the sushi rolls with soy sauce or tamari for dipping, with pickled ginger and wasabi on the side.

RECIPE TIP: For easier slicing, wet the knife with a bit of water before making each cut; this prevents the rice from sticking to the blade.

SUBSTITUTION TIP:
- Use maple syrup instead of honey for the vegan option of rice seasoning.
- Use gluten-free tamari or coconut aminos for a gluten-free dipping sauce.

NUTRITIONAL INFORMATION PER SERVING: Calories: 275; Total Fat: 14g; Total Cholesterol: 0mg; Sugar: 3g; Fiber: 7g; Protein: 4g; Sodium: 480mg; Potassium: 620mg

Savor the warmth and goodness of this Tomato Basil Elixir Soup with Creamy White Beans. It's a delightful and nourishing combination that warms your soul and nourishes your body, making it an ideal choice for a wholesome and anti-inflammatory lunch.

TOMATO BASIL ELIXIR SOUP WITH CREAMY WHITE BEANS

✅ Servings: 4   ✅ Preparation time: 15 min   ✅ Cooking time: 25 min

- 2 tablespoons extra-virgin olive oil
- 1 medium onion, chopped
- 3 cloves garlic, minced
- 1 teaspoon dried oregano
- 1 teaspoon dried basil
- 1/2 teaspoon red pepper flakes (adjust to taste)
- 28 oz (800g) canned crushed tomatoes
- 4 cups low-sodium vegetable broth

- 1 cup cooked white beans (cannellini or Great Northern), drained and rinsed
- Salt and black pepper to taste
- 1/2 cup fresh basil leaves, chopped
- 2 tablespoons nutritional yeast (optional for added flavor)
- 1/4 cup unsweetened coconut or almond milk (optional for creaminess)
- Fresh basil leaves for garnish

1. Heat the extra-virgin olive oil over medium heat in a large pot. Add the chopped onion and sauté for 3-4 minutes or until softened and translucent.
2. Add the minced garlic, dried oregano, dried basil, and red pepper flakes to the pot. Sauté for an additional 1-2 minutes until fragrant.
3. Pour in the canned crushed tomatoes and low-sodium vegetable broth. Once the mixture comes to a slight boil, reduce the heat to low and let it simmer for approximately 15-20 minutes to allow the flavors to blend.
4. Carefully blend the soup until smooth and creamy using an immersion or regular blender.
5. Return the blended soup back to the pot and stir in the cooked white beans. Add black pepper and salt to taste.
6. Add the chopped fresh basil and nutritional yeast for extra flavor if desired. Stir in the unsweetened almond or coconut milk for a creamy texture (if using).
7. Let the soup simmer for 5 min to heat the beans and blend the flavors.
8. Serve the Tomato Basil Elixir Soup with a garnish of fresh basil leaves on top.

RECIPE TIP: Strain the soup through a fine-mesh sieve after blending to remove any remaining tomato seeds or skin if you prefer a smoother consistency.

SUBSTITUTION TIP:
- Add cooked whole grains like quinoa or farro to the soup for a heartier version.
- Make a dairy-free option with unsweetened almond or coconut milk for creaminess.

NUTRITIONAL INFORMATION PER SERVING: Calories: 190; Total Fat: 7g; Total Cholesterol: 0mg; Sugar: 9g; Fiber: 10g; Protein: 7g; Sodium: 550mg; Potassium: 920mg

Enjoy the light and refreshing goodness of Cauliflower Couscous with Herb Symphony and Pomegranate Burst. This dish is a flavorful celebration of wholesome ingredients that align perfectly with your anti-inflammatory diet goals.

CAULIFLOWER COUSCOUS WITH HERB SYMPHONY AND POMEGRANATE BURST

✅ Servings: 4   ✅ Preparation time: 15 min   ✅ Cooking time: 0 min

- 1 medium head cauliflower, washed and dried
- 1/4 cup fresh parsley, finely chopped
- 2 tablespoons fresh mint, finely chopped
- 2 tablespoons fresh cilantro, finely chopped
- 1/3 cup pomegranate seeds
- 1/4 cup chopped walnuts
- 3 tablespoons extra-virgin olive oil

- 2 tablespoons lemon juice
- Salt and black pepper to taste
- 1/4 teaspoon ground cumin (optional for extra flavor)
- 1/4 teaspoon ground turmeric (optional for color)
- 1/4 teaspoon ground paprika (optional for a hint of spice)

1. Cut the cauliflower into florets, discarding the tough stem. Use a box grater or a food processor to grate the cauliflower florets into refined, rice-like grains.
2. Combine the grated cauliflower, chopped parsley, mint, and cilantro in a large mixing bowl.
3. Whisk together the extra-virgin olive oil, lemon juice, ground cumin (if using), ground turmeric (if using), and ground paprika (if using) in a separate small bowl.
4. Pour the dressing over the cauliflower mixture and toss well to combine, ensuring that all the ingredients are evenly coated.
5. Gently fold in the pomegranate seeds and chopped walnuts to add bursts of flavor and a satisfying crunch.
6. Season the cauliflower couscous with salt and black pepper to taste. Adjust the seasoning and lemon juice as needed.
7. Divide the cauliflower couscous among serving plates and garnish with additional fresh herbs, pomegranate seeds, and a drizzle of extra-virgin olive oil for a finishing touch.

RECIPE TIP: To save time, you can find pre-cut cauliflower rice at many grocery stores to save time. However, grating the cauliflower yourself allows for a fresher texture and flavor.

SUBSTITUTION TIP:
- Customize the herb blend using your favorite fresh herbs, such as basil or dill.
- If you don't have pomegranate seeds, you can use dried cranberries or raisins for a touch of sweetness.
- If you have nut allergies, exclude the walnuts or substitute with sunflower seeds for a similar nutty crunch.

NUTRITIONAL INFORMATION PER SERVING: Calories: 190; Total Fat: 15g; Total Cholesterol: 0mg; Sugar: 5g; Fiber: 6g; Protein: 4g; Sodium: 35mg; Potassium: 360mg

Elevate your lunch with the delightful flavors of Chicken and Vegetable Stir-Fry with Cashew Crunch. This dish effortlessly combines protein, fiber, and essential nutrients in a balanced and anti-inflammatory manner, making it a perfect lunch choice for anyone seeking wellness through their diet.

CHICKEN AND VEGETABLE STIR-FRY WITH CASHEW CRUNCH

✓ Servings: 4   ✓ Preparation time: 20 min   ✓ Cooking time: 15 min

For the Stuffed Zucchini:
- 1 lb (450g) boneless, thinly sliced skinless chicken breast
- 2 cups broccoli florets
- 1 red bell pepper, thinly sliced
- 1 yellow bell pepper, thinly sliced
- 1 medium carrot, julienned
- 3 green onions, sliced
- 2 cloves garlic, minced
- Salt and black pepper to taste

- 2 tablespoons extra-virgin olive oil
- 1/2 cup snow peas, ends trimmed (optional)

For the Cashew Crunch:
- 1/2 cup cashews, roughly chopped
- 1 teaspoon extra-virgin olive oil
- Pinch of salt

For the Lemon-Herb Dressing:
- 1/4 cup low-sodium soy sauce (or tamari for gluten-free)
- 2 tablespoons rice vinegar
- 1 tablespoon honey or maple syrup
- 1 teaspoon grated fresh ginger
- 1 teaspoon cornstarch

1. Whisk together in a small bowl all the sauce ingredients: soy sauce, rice vinegar, honey or maple syrup, grated ginger, and cornstarch. Set aside.
2. Heat a large skillet or wok over medium-high heat. Add the cashews and toast them for about 2 minutes, stirring frequently. Once toasted, remove the cashews from the skillet and set them aside.
3. Add 1 teaspoon of olive oil to the same skillet and heat over medium-high heat. Add the sliced chicken and cook until it's no longer pink and cooked through about 5-6 minutes. Remove the chicken from the skillet and set it aside.
4. Add one more tablespoon of olive oil to the same skillet. Add the minced garlic and sauté for about 30 seconds until fragrant. Then add the broccoli florets, bell peppers, julienned carrot, and snow peas (optional). Stir-fry the vegetables for 4-5 minutes until they're tender-crisp.
5. Return the cooked chicken to the skillet with the vegetables. Pour the prepared before sauce over the chicken and vegetables. Toss everything together to coat the ingredients in the flavorful sauce. Cook for an additional 2 minutes to heat everything through.
6. Divide the chicken and vegetable stir-fry among serving plates. Sprinkle with sliced green onions and the toasted cashews for added flavor and crunch.

RECIPE TIP: Customize the vegetable selection based on what you have on hand or prefer. Other vegetables like snap peas, zucchini, or mushrooms can also work well in this stir-fry.

SUBSTITUTION TIP: To make this dish vegan, substitute tofu for the chicken and use a plant-based alternative or maple syrup for the honey.

NUTRITIONAL INFORMATION PER SERVING: Calories: 300; Total Fat: 14g; Total Cholesterol: 45mg; Sugar: 10g; Fiber: 4g; Protein: 26g; Sodium: 600mg; Potassium: 800mg

Enjoy the flavors and nutrients of this Tuna and White Bean Salad that's both delicious and in line with the principles of an anti-inflammatory diet. This salad is packed with nutritious ingredients that provide delicious flavors and textures to nourish your body and promote your overall health.

SAVORY TUNA AND WHITE BEAN DELIGHT SALAD

✅ Servings: 2   ✅ Preparation time: 15 min   ✅ Cooking time: 0 min

- 1 can of canned Tuna, drained and flaked
- 1 can (15 oz /425g) white beans, drained and rinsed
- 1/4 red onion, finely chopped
- 1/4 cup chopped fresh parsley

- 2 tablespoons extra-virgin olive oil
- 1 tablespoon lemon juice
- 1 teaspoon Dijon mustard
- Salt and pepper, to taste
- Mixed salad greens for serving

1. Mix the drained tuna and white beans in a spacious bowl.
2. Blend the finely chopped red onion and fresh parsley into the bowl.
3. Whisk together the extra-virgin olive oil, lemon juice, Dijon mustard, salt, and pepper in a separate small bowl until the dressing is well-blended.
4. Drizzle the dressing over the tuna and white bean mixture, gently tossing the ingredients to ensure an even coating.
5. Arrange a bed of mixed salad greens on each plate for serving.
6. Carefully spoon the tuna and white bean mixture onto the salad greens.
7. If desired, add an extra sprinkle of chopped parsley for a finishing touch.

RECIPE TIP: Consider incorporating chopped almonds or walnuts into the salad to introduce an appealing crunch and boost of flavor. These nuts provide a satisfying contrast in texture and contribute healthy fats.

SUBSTITUTION TIP:
- For a vegan rendition, replace the tuna with chickpeas or cooked quinoa. Consider adding marinated tempeh or tofu to increase the protein content.
- If red onion isn't your preference, choose finely chopped scallions or shallots as a milder alternative.
- Experiment with the dressing by infusing it with herbs like basil or tarragon. To introduce a touch of sweetness, a drizzle of honey or maple syrup can be a delightful addition.

NUTRITIONAL INFORMATION PER SERVING: 330; Total Fat: 14g; Total Cholesterol: 25mg; Sugar: 2g; Fiber: 9g; Protein: 22g; Sodium: 360mg; Potassium: 650mg

Experience the delightful flavors of this Vibrant Asparagus, Tofu, and Carrot Stir-Fry, a nutritious and satisfying option that perfectly complements an anti-inflammatory diet. This stir-fry boasts a range of vivid colors and textures, making it an excellent choice for a nourishing and satisfying lunch.

VIBRANT ASPARAGUS, TOFU, AND CARROT STIR-FRY

✅ Servings: 2   ✅ Preparation time: 15 min   ✅ Cooking time: 10 min

- 8 oz (225g) firm tofu, cubed
- 1 bunch of asparagus, trimmed and cut into bite-sized pieces
- 1 cup julienned carrot
- 1 tablespoon extra-virgin olive oil
- 2 cloves garlic, minced
- 1 teaspoon fresh ginger, grated
- 2 tablespoons low-sodium soy sauce
- 1 tablespoon rice vinegar
- 1 teaspoon honey or maple syrup (optional)
- 1 teaspoon cornstarch (optional for thickening sauce)
- Salt and pepper, to taste
- Sesame seeds, for garnish
- Cooked brown rice for serving

1. Begin by pressing the tofu to remove excess moisture. Place the cubed tofu between paper towels and set a heavy object on top. Allow it to press for about 10-15 minutes.
2. Heat the extra-virgin olive oil in a wok or large skillet over medium-high heat.
3. Add the grated ginger and minced garlic to the pan, and sauté for about 1 minute until fragrant.
4. Add the cubed tofu to the pan and stir-fry for 3-4 minutes until it turns golden and crispy. Remove the tofu from the pan and set aside.
5. Add the asparagus and julienned carrot, and stir-fry in the same pan for 4-5 minutes until the vegetables are tender yet vibrant.
6. Whisk together the low-sodium soy sauce, rice vinegar, and honey or maple syrup (if using). For a thicker sauce, mix in the cornstarch.
7. Return the cooked tofu to the pan, then pour the sauce over the tofu, asparagus, and carrot. Toss everything together until well-coated and heated through, then add salt and pepper to taste.
8. Serve the stir-fry over cooked brown rice and garnish with sesame seeds for an added crunch.

RECIPE TIP: Enhance the flavor profile by adding a sprinkle of red pepper flakes to the stir-fry. This will infuse a gentle touch of heat that complements the dish wonderfully.

SUBSTITUTION TIP:

- Use maple syrup instead of honey for the sauce to create a vegan version. You can also substitute the honey with coconut sugar or agave nectar.
- If tofu isn't your preference, consider swapping it with tempeh or seitan to vary the protein source.
- Feel free to tailor the vegetables to your taste. Broccoli and snap peas are excellent alternatives or additions to this stir-fry.

NUTRITIONAL INFORMATION PER SERVING: Calories: 350; Total Fat: 15g; Total Cholesterol: 0g; Sugar: 9g; Fiber: 8g; Protein: 18g; Sodium: 710mg; Potassium: 800mg

Pamper yourself with the enticing flavors of the Mediterranean with this delightful Mediterranean Chickpea and Greens Salad that brings the Mediterranean coastline to your plate.

GREEK GODDESS CHICKPEA SALAD WITH FETA ELEGANCE

 Servings: 4   Preparation time: 15 min   Cooking time: 0 min

- 2 cups cooked chickpeas (canned or freshly cooked)
- 1 cup cucumber, diced
- 1 cup cherry tomatoes, halved
- 1/2 cup red onion, finely chopped
- 1/2 cup crumbled feta cheese, additionally extra for garnish
- 2 cups baby spinach leaves
- 1 cup arugula leaves
- 1/4 cup fresh parsley, chopped
- 1/4 cup fresh mint, chopped (optional)
- 2 tablespoons extra-virgin olive oil
- 1 tablespoon red wine vinegar
- 1 teaspoon dried oregano
- Salt and ground black pepper, to taste

1. Combine the cooked chickpeas, diced cucumber, halved cherry tomatoes, finely chopped red onion, crumbled feta cheese, baby spinach, and arugula in a large mixing bowl.
2. To create the dressing, combine the red wine vinegar, extra-virgin olive oil, dried oregano, black pepper, and salt in a small bowl.
3. Drizzle the dressing over the salad ingredients in the large mixing bowl.
4. Add the chopped fresh parsley and, if using, mint to the bowl, then gently toss all the ingredients together to combine and evenly coat with the dressing.
5. Taste the salad and adjust the seasoning if needed by adding more pepper, salt, or vinegar.
6. Divide the Mediterranean Chickpea and Greens Salad among serving plates once the flavors are well combined.
7. Garnish with a sprinkle of additional feta cheese and fresh herbs if desired, and serve immediately.

RECIPE TIP: For an extra layer of flavor, consider adding a handful of toasted pine nuts or chopped almonds to the salad.

SUBSTITUTION TIP:
- To make this vegan dish, replace feta cheese with a plant-based alternative or marinated tofu cubes.
- Feel free to swap arugula with baby kale or mixed salad greens according to your preference.
- Customize your salad with other vegetables like bell peppers, artichoke hearts, or roasted red peppers for added variety.

NUTRITIONAL INFORMATION PER SERVING: Calories: 270; Total Fat: 14g; Total Cholesterol: 20mg; Sugar: 4g; Fiber: 8g; Protein: 11g; Sodium: 420mg; Potassium: 585mg

Indulge in this nourishing salmon quinoa bowl, brimming with wholesome ingredients that support your well-being while satisfying your taste buds. This dish is an excellent option for those seeking an anti-inflammatory diet, as it is loaded with protein, healthy fats, and colorful vegetables.

SAVORY SALMON AND NUTTY QUINOA BOWL DELIGHT

 Servings: 2   Preparation time: 15 min   ✔ Cooking time: 20 min

- 2 salmon fillets
- 1 cup quinoa, rinsed and drained
- 2 cups water or low-sodium vegetable broth
- 1 red bell pepper, sliced and grilled
- 1 cup cherry tomatoes, halved
- 2 cups mixed lettuce and arugula
- 1 avocado, peeled and sliced
- Juice of 1 lemon
- Salt and black pepper, to taste
- Fresh parsley or cilantro for garnish

1. Preheat the oven to 375°F (190°C).
2. Put the salmon fillets on a baking sheet lined with parchment paper. Drizzle with salt, black pepper, olive oil, and lemon juice.
3. Bake the salmon in the preheated oven for about 15-20 minutes or until the salmon flakes easily with a fork.
4. As the salmon is baked, prepare the quinoa. Bring the water or vegetable broth to a boil in a medium saucepan. Add the quinoa and reduce the heat to low. Cover and simmer for about 15 minutes or until the quinoa is cooked and the liquid is absorbed. Fluff the quinoa with a fork.
5. In a small bowl, mash the avocado and season it with lemon juice, black pepper, and salt to make the avocado sauce.
6. Assemble the bowls: Divide the cooked quinoa between two serving bowls. Top with grilled bell pepper, cherry tomatoes, mixed lettuce, arugula, and baked salmon fillets.
7. Drizzle the avocado sauce over the bowl and garnish with fresh parsley or cilantro.
8. Serve the salmon quinoa bowls immediately, and enjoy!

RECIPE TIP: For an extra burst of flavor, sprinkle some toasted sesame seeds or crushed red pepper flakes on top of the bowl.

SUBSTITUTION TIP:
- Swap the salmon for grilled chicken, tofu, or chickpeas if you prefer a different source of protein.
- Quinoa can be substituted with brown rice or farro for a change in texture.
- If avoiding avocados, create a lemon-tahini dressing by combining tahini, lemon juice, garlic, and a touch of water.

NUTRITIONAL INFORMATION PER SERVING: Calories: 450; Total Fat: 20g; Total Cholesterol: 55mg; Sugar: 4g; Fiber: 8g; Protein: 30g; Sodium: 90mg; Potassium: 1000mg

NOURISHING
Dinners

Embrace the harmonious blend of lemon and dill as they elevate the succulent salmon to a new level of tastefulness. Enjoy the vibrant flavors and healthful benefits of this anti-inflammatory dish that's both nourishing and delectable.

LEMON-DILL HARMONY BAKED SALMON

✓ Servings: 2   ✓ Preparation time: 10 min   ✓ Cooking time: 20 min

- 2 salmon fillets (6 oz / 170g each)
- 1 lemon, thinly sliced
- 2 tablespoons fresh dill, chopped
- 2 tablespoons extra-virgin olive oil
- 1 teaspoon garlic, minced
- Salt and pepper to taste

1. Preheat the oven to 375°F (190°C). Line a baking sheet with parchment paper or lightly grease it.
2. Place the salmon fillets on the prepared baking sheet, skin-side down. Season each piece of fillet with a pinch of salt and pepper.
3. Mix the olive oil, minced garlic, and chopped dill in a small bowl. Drizzle the mixture over the salmon fillets, ensuring to coat them evenly.
4. Lay the lemon slices on the salmon fillets, arranging them in a single layer. As they bake, the lemon slices will infuse the salmon with a tangy flavor.
5. Bake the salmon in the preheated oven for about 15-20 minutes or until the salmon turns opaque and flaked easily with a fork. The cooking time may differ depending on the thickness of the fillets. If the fillets are thinner, they will cook faster.
6. Once the salmon is ready, remove it from the oven and allow it to rest for a minute before serving. This will help the flavors to meld and the juices to redistribute.

RECIPE TIP: For a burst of fresh flavor, squeeze some additional lemon juice over the baked salmon just before serving. This will enhance the citrusy notes and add a zesty kick to each bite.

SUBSTITUTION TIP:
- If you're not a fan of dill, you can use other fresh herbs like rosemary, parsley, or cilantro.
- Replace olive oil with avocado oil or melted coconut oil, if desired.
- If you're looking for a milder flavor, you can reduce the amount of garlic or omit it altogether.
- This recipe works well with other fatty fish like mackerel or trout.

NUTRITIONAL INFORMATION PER SERVING: 340; Total Fat: 23g; Total Cholesterol: 70mg; Sugar: 0g; Fiber: 0g; Protein: 31g; Sodium: 70mg; Potassium: 590mg

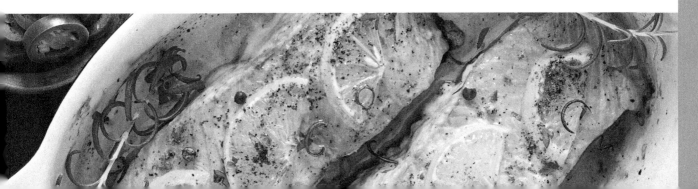

Indulge in this stir-fried masterpiece's delightful symphony of flavors as ginger and turmeric unite. This dish satisfies your taste buds and contributes to your well-being with its anti-inflammatory ingredients. Enjoy the blend of textures and vibrant colors as you savor each nutritious bite.

GINGER-TURMERIC TANGO STIR-FRIED TOFU AND VEGGIES

✔ Servings: 2   ✔ Preparation time: 10 min   ✔ Cooking time: 0 min

- 14 oz (400g) firm tofu, cubed
- 2 cups mixed vegetables (broccoli florets, bell peppers, carrots), sliced
- 2 tablespoons extra-virgin olive oil
- 1 tablespoon fresh ginger, minced
- 1 teaspoon ground turmeric
- 2 tablespoons low-sodium soy sauce
- 1 tablespoon rice vinegar
- 1 teaspoon pure maple syrup
- Salt and pepper to taste
- Chopped fresh cilantro for garnish

1. Start by pressing the cubed tofu to remove excess moisture. Place the tofu between two clean kitchen towels and gently press down to absorb the moisture. You can also place a heavy object on top of the tofu to aid in pressing.
2. Heat the olive oil over medium-high heat in a large skillet or wok. After heating the oil, add the minced ginger and sauté for about 1 minute, until fragrant.
3. Add the mixed vegetables to the skillet and stir-fry for 3-4 minutes until they soften but remain slightly crisp.
4. Push the vegetables to the side of the skillet and add the tofu cubes. Cook the tofu for about 4-5 minutes, turning occasionally, until golden and slightly crispy outside.
5. Whisk together the ground turmeric, low-sodium soy sauce, rice vinegar, and pure maple syrup in a small bowl. Pour the mixture over the vegetables and tofu into the skillet.
6. Gently toss the tofu and vegetables in the sauce, evenly coating them. Continue cooking for 1-2 minutes to allow the flavors to meld.
7. Season the stir-fry with salt and pepper to taste. Remove from heat and garnish with chopped fresh cilantro.

RECIPE TIP: Add a pinch of red pepper flakes to enhance the flavors for a hint of heat. This will complement the zesty ginger and turmeric notes in the dish.

SUBSTITUTION TIP:
- Substitute tofu with tempeh or seitan if you prefer a different protein source.
- Feel free to use any combination of your favorite vegetables, such as snap peas, zucchini, or mushrooms.
- Honey or agave nectar may be used as a substitute for pure maple syrup.

NUTRITIONAL INFORMATION PER SERVING: Calories: 210; Total Fat: 12g; Total Cholesterol: 0mg; Sugar: 5g; Fiber: 4g; Protein: 14g; Sodium: 450mg; Potassium: 420mg

These crispy herb-infused oven-roasted chicken drumsticks are a treat for your taste buds. With a perfect balance of flavors and anti-inflammatory ingredients, this dish makes for a nourishing and satisfying dinner.

CRISPY HERB-INFUSED OVEN-ROASTED CHICKEN DRUMSTICKS

✔ Servings: 4   ✔ Preparation time: 10 min   ✔ Cooking time: 40 min

- 8 chicken drumsticks
- 2 tablespoons extra-virgin olive oil
- 2 teaspoons fresh thyme leaves
- 2 teaspoons fresh rosemary leaves
- 1 teaspoon fresh sage leaves, finely chopped

- 1 teaspoon garlic powder
- 1/2 teaspoon onion powder
- 1/2 teaspoon ground turmeric
- Salt and pepper to taste
- Cooked brown rice or quinoa (for serving)

1. Preheat your oven to 400°F (200°C).
2. Combine the extra-virgin olive oil, fresh thyme leaves, fresh rosemary leaves, chopped sage, garlic powder, onion powder, ground turmeric, salt, and pepper in a small bowl. Mix well to create a fragrant herb-infused oil.
3. Pat the chicken drumsticks dry with paper towels. Place them in a large mixing bowl and drizzle the herb-infused oil over the drumsticks. Use your hands to rub the oil mixture evenly onto each drumstick, ensuring they are thoroughly coated with the aromatic herbs and spices.
4. Line a baking sheet with parchment paper or lightly grease it with olive oil to prevent sticking. Arrange the coated chicken drumsticks on the baking sheet.
5. Roast the chicken drumsticks in the preheated oven for about 35-40 minutes or until the internal temperature reaches 165°F (74°C). The skin should turn wonderfully crispy and display a golden-brown hue.
6. Once fully cooked, remove the chicken drumsticks from the oven and allow them to rest for a few minutes before serving. Accompany the crispy herb-infused drumsticks with cooked brown rice or quinoa.

RECIPE TIP: To intensify the flavor, marinate the chicken drumsticks with herb-infused oil for at least 30 minutes before roasting. This infusion time will enable the herbs and spices to permeate the meat and infuse it with delectable aromas.

SUBSTITUTION TIP:
- For a dairy-free version, omit the butter and opt for an extra drizzle of olive oil to enhance richness.
- To craft a vegan alternative, substitute the chicken drumsticks with firm tofu or tempeh and adjust the roasting time accordingly.

NUTRITIONAL INFORMATION PER SERVING: Calories: 280; Total Fat: 18g; Total Cholesterol: 105mg; Sugar: 0g; Fiber: 0g; Protein: 26g; Sodium: 85mg; Potassium: 280mg

Feel the heartwarming flavors of this nutrient-rich Butternut Bliss Chickpea Curry. This curry is packed with anti-inflammatory ingredients, making it a nourishing and satisfying dinner option.

BUTTERNUT BLISS CHICKPEA CURRY

✅ Servings: 4   ✅ Preparation time: 15 min   ✅ Cooking time: 30 min

- 2 cups cubed butternut squash
- 1 can (15 oz / 425g) chickpeas, drained and rinsed
- 1 tablespoon extra-virgin olive oil
- 1 onion, finely chopped
- 2 cloves garlic, minced
- 1 teaspoon ground turmeric
- 1 teaspoon ground cumin
- 1/2 teaspoon ground coriander

- 1/2 teaspoon ground ginger
- 1/4 teaspoon ground cinnamon
- 1/4 teaspoon cayenne pepper (adjust to taste)
- 1 can (14 oz / 400g) diced tomatoes
- 1 can (13.5 / 380g oz) full-fat coconut milk
- Salt and pepper to taste
- Fresh cilantro, chopped (for garnish)
- Cooked brown rice or quinoa (for serving)

1. Heat the olive oil over medium heat in a large skillet or pot. Add the chopped onion and sauté for 3-4 minutes until softened and translucent.
2. Add the minced garlic, turmeric, ground cumin, coriander, ginger, cinnamon, and cayenne pepper to the skillet. Cook for 1-2 minutes until fragrant.
3. Add the cubed butternut squash and chickpeas to the skillet. Stir well to coat the vegetables and chickpeas with the aromatic spices.
4. Pour in the diced tomatoes (with their juices) and full-fat coconut milk. Season with salt and pepper to taste. Stir to combine all the ingredients.
5. Heat the mixture until it gently simmers. Cover the skillet or pot with a lid and let the curry cook for about 20-25 minutes, or until the butternut squash is tender and cooked.
6. Once the curry is cooked, taste and adjust the seasoning if needed. If you prefer a thicker consistency, use a potato masher to lightly mash some butternut squash and chickpeas.
7. Serve the Butternut Bliss Chickpea Curry over cooked brown rice or quinoa.

RECIPE TIP: Add chopped cilantro or parsley while cooking or garnish when ready for a burst of freshness and color.

SUBSTITUTION TIP:
- For a vegan version, use plant-based coconut milk and skip the optional yogurt or dairy-based garnishes.
- Swap butternut squash for sweet potatoes or other winter squash varieties for a different flavor profile.

NUTRITIONAL INFORMATION PER SERVING: Calories: 320; Total Fat: 17g; Total Cholesterol: 0mg; Sugar: 8g; Fiber: 10g; Protein: 9g; Sodium: 350mg; Potassium: 750mg

Dive into a flavorful and wholesome lunch with our Shrimp Sizzle Cauliflower Rice Stir-Fry. This dish is a tasty and healthy blend of succulent shrimp, colorful veggies, and cauliflower rice.

SHRIMP & CAULIFLOWER RICE STIR-FRY PARTY

✅ Servings: 4   ✅ Preparation time: 15 min   ✅ Cooking time: 15 min

- 1 lb (450g) large shrimp, peeled and deveined
- 1 tablespoon extra-virgin olive oil
- 1 small onion, thinly sliced
- 1 red bell pepper, sliced
- 1 cup broccoli florets
- 1 cup snap peas, ends trimmed
- 3 cups cauliflower rice (store-bought or homemade)
- 2 cloves garlic, minced
- 1 tablespoon grated ginger
- 2 tablespoons low-sodium soy sauce
- 1 tablespoon sesame oil
- 1 tablespoon rice vinegar
- 1/4 teaspoon red pepper flakes (adjust to taste)
- Salt and pepper to taste
- Sesame seeds (for garnish)
- Sliced green onions (for garnish)

1. Heat the extra-virgin olive oil over medium-high heat in a large skillet or wok. Add the sliced red bell pepper and onion. Stir-fry for 2-3 minutes until the vegetables begin to soften.
2. Push the vegetables to the side of the skillet and add the shrimp. Cook the shrimp on each side for 1-2 minutes until they turn pink and opaque. Remove the shrimp from the skillet and put aside.
3. Add the broccoli florets and snap peas in the same skillet. Stir-fry for 2-3 minutes until they begin to tenderize.
4. Push the vegetables to the side and add the minced garlic and grated ginger. Cook for around 30 seconds until fragrant, then mix with the vegetables.
5. Add the cauliflower rice to the skillet. Drizzle the low-sodium soy sauce, sesame oil, and rice vinegar over the cauliflower rice. Toss everything together to combine the flavors.
6. Return the cooked shrimp back to the skillet and toss to distribute evenly throughout the stir-fry. Add pepper, salt, and red pepper flakes according to taste.
7. Continue to cook for another 2-3 minutes until the shrimp are heated through and all the ingredients are well combined.
8. Serve the Shrimp Sizzle Cauliflower Rice Stir-Fry in individual bowls. Garnish with sliced green onions & sesame seeds for an added burst of flavor and texture.

RECIPE TIP: Use lime juice to season the dish for added flavor. Add vegetables like carrots, snow peas, or baby corn to personalize your stir-fry.

SUBSTITUTION TIP: To make this dish vegetarian, replace the shrimp with tofu cubes or tempeh.

NUTRITIONAL INFORMATION PER SERVING: Calories: 220; Total Fat: 7g; Total Cholesterol: 140mg; Sugar: 5g; Fiber: 6g; Protein: 25g; Sodium: 550mg; Potassium: 650mg

Embark on a flavorful journey with this Moroccan-inspired dish that combines the goodness of quinoa and lentils. Packed with aromatic spices and colorful veggies, this cauldron of nutrition will satisfy your taste buds and support your wellness goals.

MOROCCAN QUINOA CAULDRON WITH LENTIL MAGIC

 Servings: 4   Preparation time: 15 min   Cooking time: 30 min

- 1 cup quinoa, rinsed and drained
- 1 cup green or brown lentils, rinsed and drained
- 2 tablespoons extra-virgin olive oil
- 1 onion, finely chopped
- 3 cloves garlic, minced
- 1 teaspoon ground cumin
- 1 teaspoon ground coriander
- 1/2 teaspoon ground turmeric
- 1/2 teaspoon ground cinnamon
- 1/4 teaspoon cayenne pepper (adjust to taste)
- 2 cups diced tomatoes (canned or fresh)
- 4 cups vegetable broth
- 1 cup diced carrots
- 1 cup diced bell peppers (assorted colors)
- 1 cup chopped kale or spinach
- 1/2 cup chopped fresh cilantro
- Salt and black pepper to taste
- Sliced almonds for garnish

1. Heat the olive oil over medium heat in a large pot. Add the chopped onion and sauté until translucent.
2. Stir in the minced garlic, ground cumin, coriander, turmeric, cinnamon, and cayenne pepper. Cook for about 1 minute until fragrant.
3. Add the quinoa, lentils, vegetable broth, and diced tomatoes to the pot. Heat until boiling, reduce the heat to low, cover, and let it simmer for about 15 minutes.
4. Stir in the diced carrots, bell peppers, and chopped kale or spinach. Cover the pot again and let it simmer for 10-15 minutes until the lentils and quinoa are tender and the vegetables are cooked.
5. Remove the pot from the heat Once everything is cooked and the liquid has been absorbed. Stir in the chopped cilantro and season with black pepper and salt to taste.
6. Serve the Moroccan quinoa cauldron in bowls, garnished with sliced almonds for added crunch and nuttiness.

RECIPE TIP: For added protein and flavor, stir in cooked chickpeas or diced chicken when adding the vegetables.

SUBSTITUTION TIP:
- You can substitute other hearty greens like Swiss chard or collard greens for kale or spinach.
- If you prefer a different type of nut, such as walnuts or pine nuts, feel free to use those instead of sliced almonds for the garnish.

NUTRITIONAL INFORMATION PER SERVING: Calories: 376; Total Fat: 8g; Total Cholesterol: 0mg; Sugar: 7g; Fiber: 17g; Protein: 17g; Sodium: 787mg; Potassium: 877mg

Savor the subtle taste of succulent baked cod blended with fragrant garlic and an assortment of herbs. This nourishing dinner option is a feast for the taste buds and a source of essential nutrients to support your well-being.

GARLIC-HERB ELEGANCE BAKED COD

✓ Servings: 4   ✓ Preparation time: 10 min   ✓ Cooking time: 20 min

- 4 cod fillets (about 6 oz / 170g each)
- 2 tablespoons extra-virgin olive oil
- 4 cloves garlic, minced
- 1 teaspoon dried thyme
- 1 teaspoon dried rosemary
- 1 teaspoon dried oregano
- Salt and black pepper to taste
- 1 lemon, thinly sliced
- Fresh parsley, chopped, for garnish

1. Preheat the oven to 400°F (200°C). Line a baking dish with parchment paper.
2. Place the cod fillets in the prepared baking dish and leave a small gap between each fillet.
3. Mix the extra-virgin olive oil, minced garlic, dried thyme, rosemary, dried oregano, salt, and black pepper in a small bowl.
4. Drizzle the garlic-herb mixture evenly over the cod fillets, ensuring they are well coated on all sides.
5. Place lemon slices on top of each fillet. The lemon slices infuse the cod with a zesty aroma and keep the fish moist during baking.
6. Bake the cod in the preheated oven for 15-20 minutes or until the fish is opaque and flakes easily with a fork.
7. Once cooked, remove the baking dish from the oven and garnish the cod with freshly chopped parsley for added flavor and a burst of color.
8. Serve the garlic-herb elegance baked cod alongside a generous portion of your favorite steamed vegetables, baked potatoes, or a mixed-greens salad.

RECIPE TIP: To enhance the aroma and flavor, add a vegetable broth or splash of white wine to the baking dish before placing it in the oven.

SUBSTITUTION TIP:
- If you prefer a different type of fish, such as haddock or snapper, feel free to substitute it for cod in this recipe.
- Use fresh herbs instead of dried herbs for an even more vibrant flavor. Use three times the amount of fresh herbs as the dried ones.
- To make this dish even more nutrient-rich, serve it with steamed quinoa or brown rice.

NUTRITIONAL INFORMATION PER SERVING: Calories: 260; Total Fat: 10g; Total Cholesterol: 66mg; Sugar: 0g; Fiber: 1g; Protein: 36g; Sodium: 238mg; Potassium: 761mg

Elevate your dinner with these vibrant and wholesome bell peppers stuffed with a delightful mixture of lean ground turkey, nutrient-rich quinoa, and various flavorful vegetables. This colorful dish delights the palate and supports your wellness journey.

GROUND TURKEY QUINOA-STUFFED BELL PEPPERS

✓ Servings: 4   ✓ Preparation time: 20 min   ✓ Cooking time: 40 min

- 4 bell peppers (any color), tops and seeds removed
- 1 cup quinoa, rinsed and drained
- 2 cups low-sodium vegetable broth
- 1 lb (450g) lean ground turkey
- 1 small onion, finely chopped
- 2 cloves garlic, minced
- 1 zucchini, diced
- 1 carrot, grated
- 1 teaspoon ground cumin
- 1 teaspoon paprika
- Salt and black pepper to taste
- 1 cup canned diced tomatoes, drained
- 1/4 cup chopped cilantro or fresh parsley
- Olive oil for drizzling

1. Preheat the oven to 375°F (190°C).
2. Mix the quinoa and vegetable broth in a medium saucepan. Heat until boiling, then reduce the heat to low, cover, and let simmer for 15 minutes until the quinoa is ready and the liquid is absorbed.
3. Heat a large skillet over medium heat while the quinoa cooks. Add the ground turkey & cook until browned and cooked through. Remove the turkey from the skillet and put aside.
4. Add a sprinkle of olive oil in the same skillet and sauté the chopped onion, minced garlic, diced zucchini, and grated carrot until the vegetables are tender.
5. Add the cooked ground turkey back to the skillet. Sprinkle in the ground cumin, paprika, salt, and black pepper. Mix well to combine the flavors.
6. Stir in the cooked quinoa and canned diced tomatoes. Cook for 3-4 minutes, allowing the ingredients to meld together.
7. Remove the skillet from the heat and fold in the chopped fresh parsley or cilantro.
8. Carefully stuff each bell pepper with the turkey-quinoa mixture. Move the stuffed peppers to a baking dish and place it upright. Add a small amount of olive oil over the tops of the peppers.
9. Cover the baking dish with aluminum foil and bake in the preheated oven for approximately 25-30 minutes until the peppers are tender.
10. Once cooked, take out the stuffed peppers from the oven and let them cool a bit before serving.

RECIPE TIP: For added flavor, mix your favorite spices and herbs, such as thyme, basil, or red pepper flakes, into the turkey-quinoa mixture.

SUBSTITUTION TIP: To make this dish vegetarian, substitute the ground turkey with cooked lentils or black beans.

NUTRITIONAL INFORMATION PER SERVING: Calories: 370; Total Fat: 9g; Total Cholesterol: 70mg; Sugar: 6g; Fiber: 7g; Protein: 30g; Sodium: 450mg; Potassium: 850mg

Upgrade your dinner with the fresh and invigorating flavors of this Lemon Herb Love Grilled Chicken Breast. Succulent chicken breasts are marinated in a zesty lemon and herb concoction and then grilled to perfection. This dish embodies the essence of nourishing and flavorful dining.

LEMON HERB LOVE GRILLED CHICKEN BREAST

✅ Servings: 4   ✅ Preparation time: 15 min   ✅ Cooking time: 20 min

- 4 boneless, skinless chicken breasts
- 1/4 cup extra-virgin olive oil
- Zest and juice of 1 lemon
- 2 cloves garlic, minced
- 1 teaspoon dried oregano
- 1 teaspoon dried thyme
- Salt and black pepper, to taste
- Fresh parsley, chopped, for garnish

1. Mix the extra-virgin olive oil, lemon zest, lemon juice, minced garlic, dried oregano, salt, black pepper, and dried thyme to create the marinade.
2. Place the chicken breasts in a shallow dish or a resealable plastic bag. Pour the marinade onto the chicken, ensuring each breast is coated. Seal the bag or cover the dish and refrigerate for at least 30 minutes, allowing the flavors to infuse.
3. Preheat the grill to medium-high heat.
4. Take out the chicken breasts from the marinade, and ensure any excess marinade drips off. Discard the remaining marinade.
5. Place the chicken breasts on the preheated grill and cook for about 6-8 minutes per each side until the temperature inside reaches 165°F (74°C) and the chicken is no longer pink in the center.
6. Brush the chicken with any remaining marinade for added flavor while grilling.
7. Transfer the grilled chicken breasts to a serving plate once cooked. Garnish with freshly chopped parsley for freshness and a burst of color.
8. Let the chicken rest for a few minutes before slicing and serving.

RECIPE TIP: For extra tenderness, you can use a meat mallet to gently pound the chicken breasts to an even thickness before marinating.

SUBSTITUTION TIP:
- To make this dish plant-based, substitute chicken breasts with tofu or tempeh and marinate them in the same lemon herb marinade.
- Add a touch of grated orange zest to the marinade and lemon zest for a citrusy kick.
- If you're short on time, you can marinate the chicken for at least 15 minutes; however, longer marination enhances the flavor.

NUTRITIONAL INFORMATION PER SERVING: Calories: 250; Total Fat: 12g; Total Cholesterol: 75mg; Sugar: 0g; Fiber: 0g; Protein: 32g; Sodium: 150mg; Potassium: 300mg

Embark on a culinary journey with our Seared Ahi Adventure with Sesame Ginger Glamour. This exquisite dish features succulent seared ahi tuna, complemented by a flavorful sesame ginger dressing. Indulge in this nourishing and anti-inflammatory dinner that's as delightful for your taste buds as it is for your well-being.

SEARED AHI ADVENTURE WITH SESAME GINGER GLAMOUR

✔ Servings: 2   ✔ Preparation time: 15 min   ✔ Cooking time: 5 min

- 2 ahi tuna steaks (6 oz / 170g each)
- 2 tablespoons black and white sesame seeds
- 2 tablespoons extra-virgin olive oil
- Salt and black pepper, to taste
- 1/4 cup fresh lime juice
- 2 tablespoons low-sodium soy sauce

- 1 tablespoon sesame oil
- 1 tablespoon grated fresh ginger
- 1 tablespoon honey
- 2 cups mixed greens
- 1 avocado, sliced
- 2 quartered tomatoes
- 2 tablespoons chopped fresh cilantro

1. Season the ahi tuna steaks with a pinch of salt and black pepper. Press the black and white sesame seeds onto both sides of the tuna steaks to create a flavorful crust.
2. Warm the extra-virgin olive oil in a skillet over medium-high heat until shimmering. Carefully place the tuna steaks in the skillet and sear for 1-2 minutes on each side for a rare to medium-rare doneness. Modify the cooking time based on your preferred level of doneness. Once seared, transfer the tuna steaks to a cutting board and let them rest briefly before slicing.
3. Whisk together the fresh lime juice, low-sodium soy sauce, sesame oil, grated fresh ginger, and honey (or maple syrup for a vegan option) in a small bowl to create the sesame ginger dressing.
4. Arrange a bed of mixed greens on serving plates. Top with sliced avocado and quartered tomatoes.
5. Slice the seared ahi tuna steaks into thin strips and place them on the salad.
6. Drizzle the sesame ginger dressing over the tuna and salad, allowing the flavors to mingle.
7. Garnish the dish with chopped fresh cilantro for an extra burst of freshness and flavor.

RECIPE TIP: For added texture and a nutty flavor, toss some toasted sesame seeds onto the salad before serving.

SUBSTITUTION TIP:
- Swap ahi tuna for salmon or another type of fatty fish if preferred.
- Replace honey with maple syrup to make the dressing vegan-friendly.
- Customize the greens using your favorite leafy greens, such as arugula, baby spinach, or spring mix.

NUTRITIONAL INFORMATION PER SERVING: Calories: 380; Total Fat: 23g; Total Cholesterol: 50mg; Sugar: 8g; Fiber: 6g; Protein: 28g; Sodium: 470mg; Potassium: 950mg

Elevate your dinner with the delectable Baked Lemon Garlic Delight Shrimp. This dish combines simplicity and taste perfectly, bursting with zesty lemon, aromatic garlic, and succulent shrimp flavors. While indulging in a gourmet-worthy meal, you can also enjoy its nutritional benefits and anti-inflammatory properties.

BAKED LEMON GARLIC DELIGHT SHRIMP

✔ Servings: 4   ✔ Preparation time: 15 min   ✔ Cooking time: 10 min

- 1 lb (450g) large shrimp, peeled and deveined
- 2 tablespoons extra-virgin olive oil
- 3 cloves garlic, minced
- Zest and juice of 1 lemon

- 1 teaspoon dried oregano
- Salt and black pepper, to taste
- Fresh parsley, chopped, for garnish
- Lemon wedges for serving

1. Preheat the oven to 400°F (200°C). Grease a baking dish lightly with olive oil.
2. Combine the minced garlic, olive oil, lemon zest, lemon juice, salt, black pepper, and dried oregano in a bowl. Mix well to create a marinade.
3. Add the peeled and deveined shrimp to the bowl and toss to ensure they are evenly coated with the marinade.
4. Place the shrimp onto the prepared baking dish in a single layer.
5. Bake in the oven for 8-10 minutes until the shrimp are pink and opaque.
6. Garnish with chopped fresh parsley and serve hot with lemon wedges on the side.

RECIPE TIP: Serve the Baked Lemon Garlic Delight Shrimp over a bed of quinoa or a mix of sautéed spinach and kale for a well-rounded and nutritious meal.

SUBSTITUTION TIP:
- Use fresh herbs like thyme or rosemary instead of dried oregano for a different flavor profile.
- Opt for other seafood like scallops or white fish if you prefer.
- If using frozen shrimp, thaw and pat them dry before marinating.
- Make it spicier by adding a pinch of red pepper flakes to the marinade.

NUTRITIONAL INFORMATION PER SERVING: Calories: 150; Total Fat: 7g; Total Cholesterol: 190mg; Sugar: 0g; Fiber: 0g; Protein: 23g; Sodium: 180mg; Potassium: 170mg

Spice your dinner with the vibrant and satisfying Black Bean and Sweet Potato Fiesta Enchiladas. Rolled up in corn tortillas and topped with a zesty homemade enchilada sauce, they're a flavorful delight that perfectly aligns with the principles of an anti-inflammatory diet.

BLACK BEAN AND SWEET POTATO ENCHILADAS

 Servings: 4    Preparation time: 20 min    Cooking time: 30 min

- 2 medium sweet potatoes, peeled and diced
- 1 red bell pepper, diced
- 1 yellow bell pepper, diced
- 1 can black beans (15 oz /425g), drained and rinsed
- 8 corn tortillas
- 1 cup shredded dairy-free cheese (optional)

- 1 teaspoon ground cumin
- 1 teaspoon chili powder
- Salt and black pepper, to taste
- 1 can (14 oz / 380g) crushed tomatoes
- 1 teaspoon ground cumin
- 1 teaspoon chili powder
- 1/2 teaspoon garlic powder
- 1 tablespoon extra-virgin olive oil

1. Preheat your oven to 400°F (200°C).
2. Toss the diced sweet potatoes with olive oil, chili powder, ground cumin, black pepper, and sal Spread them on a baking sheet and roast for about 20-25 minutes until the sweet potatoes ar tender and slightly caramelized.
3. Heat a drizzle of olive oil over medium heat in a large skillet. Add the diced bell peppers an sauté for 3-4 minutes, until they soften. Stir in the drained black beans and roasted swee potatoes. Season with salt and black pepper. Cook for 2 minutes, then remove from heat.
4. Combine all the ingredients for the enchilada sauce in a separate saucepan. Heat over mediur heat until it simmers, stirring occasionally. Let it cook for about 5 minutes until the flavors mel together. Adjust salt to taste.
5. To assemble the enchiladas, warm the corn tortillas slightly by wrapping them in a damp pape towel, microwaving them for a few seconds, or lightly heating them in a dry skillet.
6. Pour a small quantity of enchilada sauce onto the bottom of a baking dish.
7. Place a spoonful of the black bean and sweet potato mixture onto each tortilla, roll them up, an place them seam-side down in the baking dish.
8. Pour the remaining enchilada sauce over the rolled tortillas. Sprinkle with dairy-free cheese using.
9. Place the enchiladas in the oven and bake for 10-15 minutes until they are heated thorought and the cheese is melted and bubbly.
10. Serve the Black Bean and Sweet Potato Fiesta Enchiladas with a sprinkle of fresh cilantro an your favorite anti-inflammatory side dish.

RECIPE TIP: Add cooked quinoa or lean ground turkey to the filling for a protein boost.

SUBSTITUTION TIP: Use whole wheat tortillas or gluten-free tortillas if you prefer

NUTRITIONAL INFORMATION PER SERVING: Calories: 365; Total Fat: 6g; Total Cholesterol: 0g; Sugar: 7g; Fiber: 12g Protein: 11g; Sodium: 570mg; Potassium: 890mg

Elevate your dinner with the delightful combination of tender Rosemary-Citrus Grilled Chicken, perfectly roasted asparagus, grilled cherry tomatoes, and zesty sliced zucchini. This dish satisfies your taste buds and supports your anti-inflammatory journey.

ROSEMARY-CITRUS GRILLED CHICKEN

✔ Servings: 4   ✔ Preparation time: 15 min   ✔ Cooking time: 20 min

- 4 skinless, boneless chicken breasts (6 oz 170g each)
- 2 tablespoons extra-virgin olive oil
- 2 tablespoons freshly squeezed orange juice
- 1 tablespoon freshly squeezed lemon juice
- 2 teaspoons fresh rosemary, finely chopped
- 2 garlic cloves, minced
- Salt and black pepper, to taste
- 1 bunch of asparagus, tough ends trimmed
- 1 teaspoon olive oil
- 1 cup cherry tomatoes
- 2 zucchinis, sliced
- Zest of 1 lemon (for garnish)

1. Combine the extra-virgin olive oil, orange juice, lemon juice, minced garlic, chopped rosemary, a pinch of salt, and a dash of black pepper in a bowl. Mix well to create a flavorful marinade.
2. Put the chicken breasts in a resealable plastic bag or a shallow dish. Pour the marinade evenly over the chicken pieces, ensuring each one is well coated. After preparing the chicken, cover the dish or seal the bag. Then, place it in the refrigerator and allow it to marinate for 30 minutes. This will allow the flavors to blend.
3. Preheat your grill to medium-high heat. It is essential to clean and lightly oil the grates to avoid any sticking.
4. Take out the chicken from the marinade and let any excess drip off. Arrange the chicken breasts on the grill and cook for 5-6 minutes on each side or until the inner temperature reaches 165°F (75°C). Cooking times for chicken breasts may vary depending on their thickness. Keep a close eye on them to avoid overcooking.
5. Toss the cherry tomatoes and sliced zucchini with a pinch of salt, black pepper, and a drizzle of olive oil while the chicken grills. Place them on the grill and cook on each side for 2-3 minutes until they are lightly charred and tender.
6. While the chicken and vegetables are grilling, preheat your oven to 400°F (200°C). On a baking sheet, toss the trimmed asparagus with a pinch of black pepper, salt, and 1 teaspoon of olive oil. Roast in the oven for 10-12 minutes until the asparagus is tender yet slightly crispy.
7. Move the chicken to a serving platter Once the chicken is fully cooked. Arrange the roasted asparagus, grilled cherry tomatoes, and sliced zucchini alongside the chicken. Sprinkle the zest of one lemon over the dish for an extra burst of citrus aroma.

RECIPE TIP: For an even more pronounced citrus flavor, consider marinating the chicken for an extended period, such as 4-6 hours, in the refrigerator to allow the marinade to penetrate the meat.

SUBSTITUTION TIP: If you prefer a different protein, you can substitute the chicken breasts with boneless turkey breasts or even firm tofu slices for a vegan option.

NUTRITIONAL INFORMATION PER SERVING: Calories: 310; Total Fat: 13g; Total Cholesterol: 78mg; Sugar: 4g; Fiber: 4g; Protein: 33g; Sodium: 140mg; Potassium: 800mg

Indulge in a nourishing and flavorful Herb-Marinated Grilled Chicken Caesar Salad that brings together the goodness of marinated chicken, crisp greens, and a zesty dressing. This wholesome meal is a satisfying choice for dinner, packed with anti-inflammatory ingredients.

HERB-MARINATED GRILLED CHICKEN CAESAR SALAD

 Servings: 2   Preparation time: 10 min   Cooking time: 0 min

For Caesar Salad:
- 1 large romaine lettuce head, washed and chopped
- 1 cup cherry tomatoes, halved
- 1/2 cup grated Parmesan cheese
- 1/2 cup whole wheat croutons
- 1/4 cup extra-virgin olive oil
- 1 tablespoon Dijon mustard
- 2 tablespoons fresh lemon juice
- 1 clove garlic, minced
- Salt and black pepper, to taste

For Herb-Marinated Grilled Chicken:
- 4 boneless, skinless chicken breasts (6 oz / 170g each)
- 2 tablespoons extra-virgin olive oil
- 2 tablespoons freshly squeezed lemon juice
- 2 cloves garlic, minced
- 1 teaspoon dried oregano
- 1 teaspoon dried thyme
- Salt and black pepper, to taste

1. Combine the extra-virgin olive oil, lemon juice, dried thyme, dried oregano, minced garlic, a pinch of salt, and black pepper in a bowl. Mix well to create the marinade. Put the chicken breasts in a shallow dish or a resealable plastic bag. Pour the marinade evenly over the chicken to cover each piece. Seal the bag or cover the dish and allow the chicken to marinate in the refrigerator for a minimum of 30 minutes.

2. Preheat your grill to medium-high heat. It is essential to ensure that the grates are dirt-free and lightly coated with oil.

3. Pull the chicken from the marinade and discard the remaining marinade. Arrange the chicken breasts on the grill and cook for about 6-7 minutes on each side or until the temperature reaches 165°F (75°C). The cooking time may differ depending on the thickness of the chicken breasts. Once cooked, remove them from the grill and let them rest for a few minutes before slicing.

4. Whisk together the extra-virgin olive oil, lemon juice, Dijon mustard, minced garlic, a pinch of salt, and black pepper in a small bowl. This will be the Caesar salad dressing.

5. Combine the chopped romaine lettuce, halved cherry tomatoes, grated Parmesan cheese, and whole wheat croutons in a large mixing bowl. Pour the prepared Caesar dressing onto the salad and toss gently to cover all the ingredients.

6. Divide the Caesar salad mixture onto serving plates. Top each plate with slices of herb-marinated grilled chicken.

RECIPE TIP: For a lighter version, you can opt for grilled chicken tenders or replace the chicken with grilled tofu or chickpeas for a plant-based option.

SUBSTITUTION TIP: For dairy-free, try using nutritional yeast as a flavorful alternative to grated Parmesan cheese.

NUTRITIONAL INFORMATION PER SERVING: Calories: 390; Total Fat: 24g; Total Cholesterol: 75mg; Sugar: 3g; Fiber: 5g; Protein: 32g; Sodium: 520mg; Potassium: 570mg

Begin your day with vitality and nourishment through these delightful Rise-and-Shine Overnight Oats. A blend of wholesome oats, vibrant berries, and nutrient-rich seeds, this breakfast is a breeze to prepare and ensures sustained energy throughout your morning.

GRILLED CHICKEN AND AVOCADO TACOS WITH FRESH SALSA SAUCE AND LIME

✅ Servings: 4   ✅ Preparation time: 15 min   ✅ Cooking time: 15 min

For Grilled Chicken:
- 1 lb (450g) boneless, skinless chicken breasts
- Juice of 1 lime
- 2 tablespoons olive oil
- 2 cloves garlic, minced
- 1 teaspoon ground cumin
- 1/2 teaspoon chili powder
- Salt and black pepper, to taste

For Fresh Salsa Sauce:
- 1 cup cherry tomatoes, diced
- 1/4 cup red onion, finely chopped
- 1/4 cup fresh cilantro, chopped
- Juice of 1 lime
- Salt and black pepper, to taste

For Tacos:
- 8 small corn or whole wheat tortillas
- 2 ripe avocados, sliced
- Lime wedges for serving

1. Whisk together lime juice, olive oil, minced garlic, chili powder, ground cumin, salt, and black pepper in a bowl. Put the chicken breasts into the marinade, ensuring they're well-coated. Allow to marinate for at least 20 minutes.
2. Preheat a grill or grill pan over medium-high heat. Clean and lightly oil the grates.
3. Remove the chicken from the marinade and grill for 6-7 minutes per side or until the internal temperature reaches 165°F (75°C). Once cooked, let the chicken rest for a few minutes before slicing.
4. Combine diced cherry tomatoes, chopped red onion, chopped cilantro, lime juice, salt, and black pepper in a bowl. Mix well to create the fresh salsa sauce.
5. Heat the tortillas on the grill or in a dry skillet for 10-15 seconds per side until warm and pliable.
6. Place a few slices of grilled chicken onto each tortilla. Top with avocado slices and a generous spoonful of fresh salsa sauce. Squeeze a lime wedge over each taco.
7. Serve the Grilled Chicken and Avocado Tacos with Fresh Salsa Sauce and Lime immediately, allowing your taste buds to savor the delicious combination of flavors.

RECIPE TIP: For an extra kick of flavor, you can sprinkle some crumbled feta cheese or a drizzle of Greek yogurt on top of your tacos before serving.

SUBSTITUTION TIP: Swap chicken with grilled tofu or portobello mushrooms for a vegetarian version.

NUTRITIONAL INFORMATION PER SERVING: Calories: 400; Total Fat: 18g; Total Cholesterol: 70mg; Sugar: 3g; Fiber: 8g; Protein: 30g; Sodium: 350mg; Potassium: 850mg

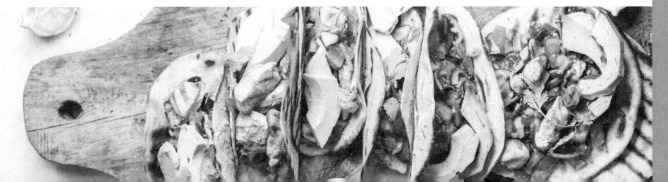

SATISFYING

Snacks

The cozy flavors of these spiced almonds and cashews wrap you in a warm embrace of comfort. A blend of aromatic spices coats the crunchy nuts, making this snack a perfect companion for your anti-inflammatory journey.

SPICED ALMONDS AND CASHEWS

 Servings: 4   Preparation time: 10 min   Cooking time: 15 min

- 1 cup raw almonds
- 1 cup raw cashews
- 1 tablespoon extra-virgin olive oil
- 1 teaspoon ground cumin

- 1/2 teaspoon ground turmeric
- 1/2 teaspoon ground cinnamon
- 1/4 teaspoon cayenne pepper (adjust to taste)
- Salt to taste

1. Preheat your oven to 325°F (165°C) and line a baking sheet with parchment paper.
2. In a mixing bowl, combine the almonds and cashews.
3. Drizzle the extra-virgin olive oil over the nuts and toss to coat them evenly.
4. Mix the ground cumin, turmeric, cayenne pepper, ground cinnamon, and a pinch of salt in a separate bowl.
5. Sprinkle the spice mixture over the nuts and toss well to ensure they are coated with the aromatic blend.
6. Spread the spiced almonds and cashews in a single layer on the baking sheet.
7. Roast the nuts in the oven for about 15 minutes, stirring once halfway through to ensure even roasting.
8. Remove the nuts from the oven and cool completely before putting them in an airtight container.

RECIPE TIP: Store the spiced almonds and cashews in an airtight container to keep them fresh and crunchy for a satisfying snack on the go.

SUBSTITUTION TIP:
- If you prefer a milder spice level, you can reduce the amount of cayenne pepper or omit it entirely.
- Feel free to experiment with other ground spices like paprika, ginger, or nutmeg to create your unique flavor profile.
- Customize the nut blend by adding dried fruits like cranberries or raisins for a touch of sweetness and contrast in texture.

NUTRITIONAL INFORMATION PER SERVING: Calories: 220; Total Fat: 18g; Total cholesterol: 0mg; Sugar: 2g; Fiber: 4g; Protein: 7g; Sodium: 60mg; Potassium: 260mg

Vibrant Crunch Hummus with a rainbow of colorful veggie sticks. Creamy hummus meets crispy and fresh vegetables for a satisfying, nutrient-packed snack that bursts with flavor and health benefits.

VIBRANT CRUNCH HUMMUS WITH COLORFUL VEGGIE STICKS

 Servings: 4   Preparation time: 15 min   Cooking time: 0 min

For the Hummus:
- 1 can (15 ounces) chickpeas, drained and rinsed
- 1/4 cup tahini
- 3 tablespoons extra-virgin olive oil
- 2 cloves garlic, minced
- 2 tablespoons lemon juice
- 1/2 teaspoon ground cumin
- Salt and black pepper, to taste
- Water (as needed to achieve desired consistency)

For the Veggie Sticks:
- 1 cup baby carrots, washed and peeled
- 1 cup cucumber, sliced into sticks
- 1 cup bell peppers (assorted colors), sliced into strips
- 1 cup celery, cut into sticks

1. Combine the chickpeas, tahini, extra-virgin olive oil, minced garlic, lemon juice, ground cumin, salt, and black pepper in a food processor. Blend until smooth and creamy. Add a tablespoon of water at a time to achieve your desired consistency. Taste and adjust seasonings as necessary.
2. Wash, peel, and slice the baby carrots, cucumber, bell peppers, and celery into sticks. Arrange them on a serving platter.
3. Transfer the creamy hummus to a bowl and place it in the center of the veggie sticks platter. Garnish the hummus with a drizzle of extra-virgin olive oil and a sprinkle of paprika if desired.

RECIPE TIP: To enhance the flavor of your hummus, you can experiment with adding a pinch of ground turmeric or smoked paprika for a unique twist.

SUBSTITUTION TIP:
- If using dried chickpeas, soak and cook them according to package instructions before making the hummus.
- If you're out of tahini, replace it with almond or cashew butter.
- Feel free to substitute or add other colorful veggies such as radishes, cherry tomatoes, or jicama sticks.
- In addition to veggie sticks, you can serve the hummus with whole-grain pita bread, whole-wheat crackers, or whole-grain tortilla chips for added variety.

NUTRITIONAL INFORMATION PER SERVING: Calories: 220; Total Fat: 12g; Total Cholesterol: 0mg; Sugar: 6g; Fiber: 8g; Protein: 6g; Sodium: 280mg; Potassium: 450mg

Elevate your dinner with the delectable Baked Lemon Garlic Delight Shrimp. This dish combines simplicity and taste perfectly, bursting with zesty lemon, aromatic garlic, and succulent shrimp flavors. While indulging in a gourmet-worthy meal, you can also enjoy its nutritional benefits and anti-inflammatory properties.

AVOCADO GUACAMOLE WITH CORN NACHOS

 Servings: 6   Preparation time: 15 min   Cooking time: 15 min

- 3 ripe avocados, peeled and pitted
- 1 small red onion, finely diced
- 1-2 fresh jalapeño peppers, finely diced (adjust to spice preference)
- 1/4 cup fresh cilantro, chopped
- Juice of 2 limes
- Salt and pepper to taste
- 6 whole grain corn tortillas
- Olive oil (for brushing)
- Ground cumin and paprika (for seasoning)

1. Use a fork to mash the ripe avocados in a mixing bowl until they're creamy yet slightly textured.
2. Incorporate finely diced red onion, jalapeño peppers, and chopped cilantro into the mashed avocados.
3. Squeeze the juice of two limes into the mixture to infuse it with zesty notes.
4. Season the blend with salt and pepper, ensuring an even distribution of flavors.
5. Preheat the oven to 350°F (175°C).
6. To make the whole-grain corn nachos, brush both sides of the whole-grain corn tortillas lightly with olive oil.
7. Stack the tortillas and cut them into wedges or triangles using a sharp knife or a pizza cutter.
8. Arrange the cut tortillas on a baking sheet in a single layer, ensuring they don't overlap.
9. Lightly sprinkle ground cumin and paprika over the tortilla wedges for added flavor.
10. Bake the tortillas in the oven for 10-15 minutes or until they turn crisp and golden brown.
11. Allow the homemade whole-grain corn nachos to cool before serving them alongside the creamy avocado guacamole.

RECIPE TIP: For extra flavor, add a sprinkle of nutritional yeast to the whole-grain corn nachos before baking. It imparts a delightful cheesy taste without compromising the anti-inflammatory aspects of the recipe.

SUBSTITUTION TIP:
- While the creamy avocado guacamole is already packed with flavors, feel free to get creative with toppings. Add diced tomatoes, finely chopped red bell peppers, or even a sprinkle of crumbled feta cheese for an extra burst of texture and taste.
- To make this recipe fully vegan, ensure that any optional toppings or additions are plant-based. You can also use a dairy-free yogurt or sour cream alternative for a vegan-friendly dip.

NUTRITIONAL INFORMATION PER SERVING (GUACAMOLE ONLY): Calories: 160; Total Fat: 14g; Total cholesterol: 0mg; Sugar: 1g; Fiber: 7g; Protein: 2g; Sodium: 10mg; Potassium: 550mg

Experience the delightful crunch of kale leaves seasoned with a touch of sea salt. These chips are not only satisfying but also a nutritious and anti-inflammatory alternative to traditional chips.

CRISPY SEA SALT BAKED KALE CHIPS

✓ Servings: 2   ✓ Preparation time: 10 min   ✓ Cooking time: 15 min

- 1 bunch of kale, stems removed and torn into bite-sized pieces
- 1 tablespoon extra-virgin olive oil
- Sea salt, to taste

1. Preheat your oven to 300°F (150°C).
2. Wash the kale leaves thoroughly and dry them completely using a clean kitchen towel or paper towel. Ensure that the leaves are free of excess moisture to achieve maximum crispiness.
3. Drizzle the torn kale leaves with extra-virgin olive oil in a large mixing bowl. Gently massage the leaves with your hands to ensure they are evenly coated with the oil. Massaging the leaves helps to soften them and enhances the flavor.
4. Put parchment paper onto the baking sheet. Arrange the oiled kale leaves in a single layer on the baking sheet, ensuring they are not crowded. This helps to ensure even baking and crispiness.
5. Place the baking sheet in the oven and bake for 12-15 minutes until the kale leaves are crispy and slightly golden around the edges. Keep a close eye on them to prevent burning.
6. After removing the kale chips from the oven, add a pinch of sea salt to them while they are still warm. The residual heat will help the salt adhere to the chips.
7. Allow the kale chips to cool on the baking sheet for a few minutes to become even crispier. Once they are cool to the touch, transfer them to a bowl and enjoy your guilt-free, nutrient-packed snack.

RECIPE TIP: Feel free to get creative with seasonings! Add a sprinkle of nutritional yeast, cayenne pepper, or garlic powder for flavor variation.

SUBSTITUTION TIP:
- Use other leafy greens like collard or Swiss chard if kale is unavailable.
- Substitute extra-virgin olive oil with avocado or coconut oil for a different flavor profile.
- Instead of sea salt, you can use Himalayan pink salt or a seasoned salt blend for added depth of flavor.

NUTRITIONAL INFORMATION PER SERVING: Calories: 60; Total Fat: 4g; Total Cholesterol: 0mg; Sugar: 0g; Fiber: 2g; Protein: 2g; Sodium: 150mg; Potassium: 240mg

These chips offer a satisfying and flavorful snack option that's both crispy and wholesome! With a hint of aromatic rosemary, these chips will satisfy your cravings and provide a dose of anti-inflammatory goodness.

ROSEMARY KISSED BAKED SWEET POTATO CHIPS

✔ Servings: 4   ✔ Preparation time: 15 min   ✔ Cooking time: 25 min

- 2 medium sweet potatoes, washed and scrubbed
- 2 tablespoons extra-virgin olive oil
- 1/2 teaspoon sea salt
- 1 tablespoon fresh rosemary leaves, finely chopped
- 1/4 teaspoon ground black pepper

1. Preheat your oven to 375°F (190°C) and place parchment paper onto two baking sheets.
2. Slice the sweet potatoes into thin, even rounds using a mandoline or a sharp knife. It's best to aim for uniform thickness to ensure even baking.
3. Toss the sweet potato slices with extra-virgin olive oil in a large bowl, ensuring each piece is lightly coated.
4. Sprinkle the finely chopped fresh rosemary leaves over the sweet potato slices. Add the sea salt and black pepper as well.
5. Gently toss the sweet potato slices again, ensuring that the rosemary, salt, and pepper are evenly distributed.
6. Arrange the seasoned sweet potato slices in a single layer on the baking sheets, ensuring they don't overlap.
7. Bake in the oven for 20-25 minutes, flipping the chips halfway through the baking time. Keep an eye on them, as they can quickly turn from golden to burnt.
8. Once the chips are golden and crisp, remove them from the oven and let them cool on the baking sheets for a few minutes. As they cool, they will become even crispier.
9. Serve the rosemary-kissed baked sweet potato chips as a satisfying and flavorful snack.

RECIPE TIP: For extra flavor, infuse the olive oil with rosemary before tossing the sweet potato slices. Heat the olive oil at low heat with a sprig of fresh rosemary until it becomes fragrant. Remove the rosemary sprig before drizzling the infused oil over the sweet potato slices. This step adds an aromatic touch that elevates the overall taste of your baked chips.

SUBSTITUTION TIP:
- If you're not a fan of rosemary, try substituting it with thyme, oregano, or even a pinch of smoked paprika for a different flavor profile.
- Lightly sprinkle the sweet potato slices with cinnamon before baking for a slightly sweeter version.

NUTRITIONAL INFORMATION PER SERVING: Calories: 120; Total Fat: 7g; Total Cholesterol: 0g; Sugar: 5g; Fiber: 3g; Protein: 1g; Sodium: 250mg; Potassium: 190mg

Indulge in guilt-free snacking with Cashew Cream Baked Zucchini Fries! These crispy and flavorful zucchini fries are coated in a nutty cashew cream mixture, baked to perfection, and ready to satisfy your cravings without compromising your health.

CASHEW CREAM BAKED ZUCCHINI FRIES

 Servings: 4   Preparation time: 20 min   Cooking time: 25 min

For the Cashew Cream:
- 1 cup raw cashews, soaked in water for 2 hours
- 1/4 cup water
- 1 tablespoon nutritional yeast
- 1 teaspoon lemon juice
- 1/2 teaspoon garlic powder
- Salt and pepper to taste

For the Zucchini Fries:
- 2 large zucchinis, cut into fry-shaped sticks
- 1 cup gluten-free breadcrumbs
- 1 teaspoon paprika
- 1/2 teaspoon onion powder
- 1/4 teaspoon cayenne pepper (optional, for a hint of heat)
- Salt and pepper to taste
- Cooking spray

1. Preheat oven to 425°F (220°C) and place parchment paper onto a baking sheet.
2. Drain and rinse the soaked cashews. Combine the soaked cashews, water, nutritional yeast, lemon juice, garlic powder, salt, and pepper in a blender. Blend until smooth and creamy. This will be your cashew cream coating.
3. Mix the gluten-free breadcrumbs, onion powder, salt, pepper, paprika, and cayenne pepper (if using) in a shallow bowl.
4. Dip each zucchini stick into the cashew cream, ensuring it's fully coated.
5. Coat the zucchini stick with breadcrumbs by rolling it in the mixture and gently pressing it to ensure the breadcrumbs stick.
6. Place the coated zucchini fries on the baking sheet, leaving space between each fry.
7. Lightly spray the zucchini fries with cooking spray to help them crisp up in the oven.
8. Bake in the oven for 20-25 minutes until the fries are golden brown and crispy. Turn them over halfway through baking for even browning.
9. Remove from the oven and let the zucchini fries cool slightly before serving.

RECIPE TIP: Add a pinch of your favorite dried herbs, such as thyme or rosemary, to the breadcrumb mixture for a flavor variation.

SUBSTITUTION TIP:
- Replace the cashew dip with a dairy-free yogurt-based alternative for those with nut allergies. This creamy swap still offers a delightful contrast to the crispy zucchini fries.
- Create an enticing texture by rolling your zucchini sticks in a mixture of sesame seeds and whole-grain breadcrumbs before baking.

NUTRITIONAL INFORMATION PER SERVING: Calories: 230; Total Fat: 14g; Total Cholesterol: 0g; Sugar: 4g; Fiber: 3g; Protein: 9g; Sodium: 240mg; Potassium: 440mg

COMFORTING
Soups

Indulge in the comforting embrace of homemade chicken and vegetable broth, lovingly crafted with aromatic herbs and nourishing ingredients. This revitalizing elixir warms the soul and provides a wealth of nutrients to boost your well-being. Prepare to sip on a bowl of goodness as delicious as healing.

CHICKEN AND VEGETABLE BROTH WITH FRESH HERBS

✓ Servings: 6   ✓ Preparation time: 15 min   ✓ Cooking time: 1 hour

- 1 whole organic chicken, quartered
- 2 carrots, chopped
- 2 celery stalks, chopped
- 1 onion, quartered
- 4 cloves garlic, smashed
- 1 teaspoon turmeric powder
- 1 teaspoon black peppercorns
- 2 bay leaves
- 4 sprigs fresh thyme
- 4 sprigs fresh rosemary
- 8 cups water
- Salt, to taste

1. Cover the chicken quarters with water in a large stockpot. Bring to a boil over high heat.
2. Reduce the heat to a gentle simmer as the water boils. Skim off any foam that rises to the surface.
3. Add the chopped carrots, celery, onion, smashed garlic, turmeric powder, black peppercorns, bay leaves, fresh thyme, and fresh rosemary.
4. Cover the pot and let the broth simmer for about 1 hour, occasionally skimming the surface to ensure clarity.
5. After simmering, remove the chicken and vegetables from the pot using a slotted spoon and set them aside. Discard the bay leaves and herb sprigs.
6. Strain the broth into a clean container using a fine mesh strainer or cheesecloth — season with salt to taste.
7. Shred the cooked chicken meat and chop the cooked vegetables. Add them back to the strained broth.
8. Reheat the broth and enjoy the comforting goodness of nourishing chicken and vegetables.

RECIPE TIP: For added richness, you can roast the quartered chicken in the oven for 15 minutes before adding it to the stockpot.

SUBSTITUTION TIP:
- Replace the chicken with tofu or tempeh for a plant-based version. Use vegetable broth as the base and add extra vegetables for depth.
- Customize the flavor using different fresh herbs. Try thyme, rosemary, sage, or parsley to infuse the broth with delightful herbal notes.

NUTRITIONAL INFORMATION PER SERVING: Calories: 150; Total Fat: 6g; Total cholesterol 50mg; Sugar: 2g; Fiber 1; Protein 18g; Sodium 150mg; Potassium 350mg

Enjoy the velvety goodness of our Creamy Broccoli and Almond Soup. This nourishing blend of tender broccoli and nutty almonds creates a satisfyingly creamy, comforting, anti-inflammatory texture.

CREAMY BROCCOLI AND ALMOND SOUP

 Servings: 4   Preparation time: 15 min   Cooking time: 25 min

- 2 cups broccoli florets
- 1 tablespoon extra-virgin olive oil
- 1 onion, chopped
- 2 cloves garlic, minced
- 1/2 cup raw almonds
- 4 cups vegetable broth

- 1 teaspoon ground turmeric
- 1/2 teaspoon ground cumin
- 1/4 teaspoon ground nutmeg
- Salt and pepper to taste
- Sliced almonds, toasted, for garnish

1. Steam or boil broccoli florets until tender. Put aside.
2. Heat olive oil over medium heat in a large pot. Add chopped onion and sauté until translucent.
3. Stir in minced garlic and cook for 1 minute until fragrant.
4. Add raw almonds and cook for 2 minutes, stirring occasionally.
5. Pour in vegetable broth and add steamed broccoli. Bring to a gentle boil.
6. Reduce heat and simmer for 10 minutes. Allow the soup to cool slightly.
7. Carefully blend the soup until smooth and creamy using a blender or immersion blender.
8. Return the blended soup to the pot and stir in ground turmeric, ground cumin, ground nutmeg, salt, and pepper. Heat gently until warmed through.
9. Serve hot, garnished with toasted sliced almonds.

RECIPE TIP: Sprinkle some toasted pumpkin or sunflower seeds to add a satisfying crunch.

SUBSTITUTION TIP:
- Use almond milk instead of raw almonds for a nut-free version.
- Replace ground turmeric with curry powder for a different flavor profile.
- Add a drizzle of extra-virgin olive oil before serving for extra richness.
- Experiment with other greens like spinach or kale for a variation.

NUTRITIONAL INFORMATION PER SERVING: Calories: 208; Total Fat: 14g; Total Cholesterol: 0mg; Sugar: 3g; Fiber: 5g; Protein: 7g; Sodium: 683mg; Potassium: 462mg

Feel the comforting flavors of earthy mushrooms and fragrant thyme with this creamy soup. A bowl of warmth and nourishment that's perfect for satisfying snack cravings.

CREAMY MUSHROOM AND THYME SOUP

✔ Servings: 4   ✔ Preparation time: 15 min   ✔ Cooking time: 25 min

- 1 lb (450g) mushrooms, sliced
- 1 onion, finely chopped
- 2 cloves garlic, minced
- 2 tbsp extra-virgin olive oil
- 4 cups vegetable broth
- 1 tsp dried thyme
- 1 cup unsweetened almond milk
- Salt and pepper to taste
- Fresh oregano for garnish

1. Heat the olive oil over medium heat in a large pot. Add the chopped onion and sauté until translucent, about 3 minutes. Add the minced garlic and sauté for an additional 1 minute.
2. Add the sliced mushrooms to the pot and cook until they release moisture and start to brown, about 5-7 minutes.
3. Pour in the vegetable broth and dried thyme. Bring the mixture to a gentle simmer, then cover and let it cook for about 15 minutes to allow the flavors to meld.
4. Use an immersion blender to carefully blend the soup until smooth. Alternatively, let the soup cool slightly and blend in batches using a regular blender.
5. Return the blended soup to the pot and stir the almond milk. Season with salt and pepper to taste. Heat the soup gently over low heat, stirring occasionally, for about 5 minutes to warm through.
6. Serve the creamy mushroom and thyme soup hot, garnished with fresh oregano, for an extra burst of aroma and flavor.

RECIPE TIP: Add cooked quinoa or brown rice before serving for a heartier soup version. This will not only provide a satisfying texture but also extra nutrients.

SUBSTITUTION TIP:
- To make the soup dairy-free, use unsweetened coconut or oat milk instead of almond milk.
- Feel free to experiment with different types of mushrooms, such as cremini, shiitake, or portobello, to vary the flavor and texture.
- If you're a fan of fresh herbs, you can substitute fresh oregano for dried. Just use about twice the amount of dried oregano.

NUTRITIONAL INFORMATION PER SERVING: Calories: 120; Total Fat: 8g; Total Cholesterol: 0mg; Sugar: 4g; Fiber: 3g Protein: 3g; Sodium: 580mg; Potassium: 440mg

Elevate your lunchtime with this nourishing soup's rich flavors of roasted eggplant and ripe tomatoes. Enjoy the warm and comforting bowl that's a delightful way to curb your cravings.

ROASTED EGGPLANT AND TOMATO SOUP

✅ Servings: 4   ✅ Preparation time: 15 min   ✅ Cooking time: 30 min

- 1 large eggplant, cut into chunks
- 4 ripe tomatoes, quartered
- 1 onion, chopped
- 3 cloves garlic, minced
- 2 tbsp extra-virgin olive oil
- 4 cups vegetable broth
- 1 tsp dried basil
- Salt and pepper to taste
- Fresh basil leaves for garnish

1. Preheat your oven to 400°F (200°C). Place the eggplant chunks and quartered tomatoes on a baking sheet. Add a few drops of olive oil and a sprinkle of salt and pepper. Roast in the oven for about 20 minutes or until the vegetables are tender and slightly caramelized.
2. Heat a tablespoon of olive oil over medium heat in a large pot. Add the chopped onion and sauté until it becomes translucent, about 3 minutes. Add the minced garlic and sauté for an additional 1 minute.
3. Add the roasted eggplant and tomatoes to the pot, along with the vegetable broth and dried basil. Bring the mixture to a simmer and cook for 10 minutes to allow the flavors to meld.
4. Use an immersion blender to carefully blend the soup until smooth. Alternatively, allow the soup to cool slightly and blend in batches using a regular blender.
5. Return the blended soup to the pot and gently heat it over low heat for 5 minutes to ensure it's warmed through.
6. Season with salt and pepper to taste. Ladle the roasted eggplant and tomato soup into bowls and garnish with fresh basil leaves for an extra flavor.

RECIPE TIP: Stir in a splash of unsweetened coconut or almond milk before serving for a creamier texture.

SUBSTITUTION TIP:
- Feel free to experiment with other herbs for a different flavor profile. Fresh oregano or thyme can work well in place of dried basil.
- Add cooked quinoa or brown rice when serving to make the soup heartier.
- Grill the eggplant and tomatoes instead of roasting them in the oven if you prefer a smokier flavor.

NUTRITIONAL INFORMATION PER SERVING: Calories: 120; Total Fat: 6g; Total Cholesterol: 0mg; Sugar: 9g; Fiber: 5g; Protein: 3g; Sodium: 600mg; Potassium: 680mg

Dive into the luxurious creaminess of this spinach and avocado soup, brimming with the goodness of nutrient-packed ingredients. A bowlful of comfort that's perfect for satisfying your snack cravings in a health-conscious way.

CREAMY SPINACH AND AVOCADO SOUP

✅ Servings: 4　　✅ Preparation time: 15 min　　✅ Cooking time: 15 min

- 2 ripe avocados, peeled and pitted
- 4 cups fresh spinach leaves
- 1 small onion, chopped
- 2 cloves garlic, minced
- 4 cups vegetable broth

- 1 cup unsweetened almond milk
- 2 tbsp extra-virgin olive oil
- 1 tsp dried thyme
- Salt and pepper to taste
- Fresh greens for garnish

1. Heat the olive oil over medium heat in a large pot. Add the chopped onion and sauté until it becomes translucent, about 3 minutes. Add the minced garlic and sauté for an additional 1 minute.
2. Add the fresh spinach leaves to the pot and cook for 2-3 minutes, until wilted.
3. Add the vegetable broth to the mixture and heat it until it simmers. Let it cook for about 5 minutes to allow the flavors to meld.
4. Place the peeled and pitted avocados in a blender while the soup simmer. Add the cooked spinach mixture and unsweetened almond milk. Blend until smooth and creamy.
5. Return the blended mixture to the pot and gently heat it over low heat for 5 minutes, stirring occasionally.
6. Season the soup with dried thyme, salt, and pepper. Stir well to combine and ensure an even distribution of flavors.
7. Ladle the creamy spinach and avocado soup into bowls. Garnish with fresh greens for an extra flavor.

RECIPE TIP: For added richness, stir in a teaspoon of extra-virgin olive oil or a dollop of plain Greek yogurt before serving.

SUBSTITUTION TIP:
- To make the soup nut-free, you can substitute unsweetened coconut milk for almond milk and omit the sliced almonds for garnish.
- Feel free to customize the flavor by adding a pinch of nutmeg or a dash of lemon juice.
- Add cooked quinoa or brown rice to the soup for a heartier version when serving.

NUTRITIONAL INFORMATION PER SERVING: Calories: 280; Total Fat: 22g; Total Cholesterol: 0mg; Sugar: 3g; Fiber: 8g; Protein: 5g; Sodium: 700mg; Potassium: 850mg

Indulge in the velvety richness of this creamy butternut squash and apple soup, a delightful combination of wholesome ingredients that will keep you cozy and satisfied.

CREAMY BUTTERNUT SQUASH AND APPLE SOUP

✔ Servings: 6   ✔ Preparation time: 15 min   ✔ Cooking time: 30 min

- 1 butternut squash (medium), peeled, seeded, and diced
- 2 apples, peeled, cored, and diced
- 1 small onion, chopped
- 2 cloves garlic, minced
- 4 cups vegetable broth

- 1 cup unsweetened almond milk
- 2 tbsp extra-virgin olive oil
- 1 tsp ground cinnamon
- 1/2 tsp ground nutmeg
- Salt and pepper to taste
- Chopped fresh parsley for garnish

1. Heat the olive oil over medium heat in a large pot. Add the chopped onion and sauté until it becomes translucent, about 3 minutes. Add the minced garlic and sauté for an additional 1 minute.
2. Add the diced butternut squash and apples to the pot. Cook for 5 minutes, stirring occasionally, until they soften.
3. Pour in the vegetable broth and bring the mixture to a boil. Reduce the heat and let it simmer for 15-20 minutes or until the squash and apples are tender.
4. Using an immersion blender or transferring in batches to a regular blender, blend the cooked mixture until smooth and creamy.
5. Return the blended soup to the pot and stir in the unsweetened almond milk, ground cinnamon, and ground nutmeg. Heat the soup on low heat for 5 minutes, stirring occasionally.
6. Season the soup with salt and pepper, adjusting the seasonings according to your preferences.
7. Ladle the creamy butternut squash and apple soup into bowls. Garnish with chopped fresh parsley for a burst of color and freshness.

RECIPE TIP: To add a hint of sweetness, drizzle a teaspoon of pure maple syrup on top of each serving before garnishing with parsley.

SUBSTITUTION TIP:
- Swap unsweetened almond milk with coconut milk if you are nut-free.
- If you prefer a spicier flavor profile, sprinkle a cayenne pepper or chili powder pinch during cooking.
- Add a handful of cooked quinoa or brown rice to each serving to make it heartier.

NUTRITIONAL INFORMATION PER SERVING: Calories: 180; Total Fat: 7g; Total Cholesterol: 0mg; Sugar: 10g; Fiber: 5g; Protein: 3g; Sodium: 500mg; Potassium: 450mg

Experience the enchanting blend of garlic and lime as they serenade your palate, perfectly complementing the tender salmon and asparagus. This dish is a testament to the magic that can happen when simple, wholesome ingredients harmonize.

GARLIC-LIME SALMON WITH ASPARAGUS

✓ Servings: 4   ✓ Preparation time: 15 min   ✓ Cooking time: 15 min

- 4 salmon fillets (6 oz / 170g each), skin-on
- 1 lb (450g) asparagus, tough ends trimmed
- 3 cloves garlic, minced
- Zest of 1 lime
- Juice of 1 lime
- 2 tbsp extra-virgin olive oil
- Salt and pepper to taste
- Fresh dill for garnish

1. Preheat the oven to 400°F (200°C).
2. Combine the minced garlic, extra-virgin olive oil, lime juice, and zest in a small bowl to create the marinade. Season with salt and pepper to taste.
3. Put the salmon fillets in a shallow dish and evenly pour the marinade. Allow the salmon to marinate for 10 minutes.
4. Arrange the trimmed asparagus on a baking sheet while the salmon marinades. Drizzle some olive oil, and season with salt and pepper.
5. Transfer the marinated salmon fillets to the baking sheet, skin-side down, next to the asparagus. Pour any remaining marinade over the salmon.
6. Place the salmon in the oven and bake for 12-15 minutes until it easily flakes with a fork and the asparagus is tender yet slightly crisp.
7. Once ready, take it out from the oven and serve the garlic-lime symphony salmon over a bed of asparagus. Garnish with fresh dill.

RECIPE TIP: Place the salmon fillets on parchment paper before baking to prevent the skin from sticking to the baking sheet.

SUBSTITUTION TIP:
- Swap salmon for another fatty fish like mackerel or trout to enjoy similar health benefits.
- For a vegetarian option, replace salmon with thick slices of tofu or portobello mushrooms, adjusting the cooking time as needed.

NUTRITIONAL INFORMATION PER SERVING: Calories: 350; Total Fat: 22g; Total Cholesterol: 80mg; Sugar: 2g; Fiber: 2g; Protein: 30g; Sodium: 80mg; Potassium: 750mg

Savor the symphony of succulent shrimp, rich butter, and vibrant lemon in this dish that's as delightful to cook as it is to relish. The combination of fresh ingredients creates a harmonious balance of flavors, making it a go-to recipe for both weeknight dinners and special occasions.

LEMON BUTTER MAGIC FOR SUCCULENT SHRIMP

✅ Servings: 4 ✅ Preparation time: 10 min ✅ Cooking time: 10 min

- 1 lb (450g) large shrimp, peeled and deveined
- 3 tbsp unsalted butter
- 2 cloves garlic, minced
- Zest and juice of 1 lemon
- Salt and pepper to taste

1. Pat the shrimp dry with paper towels and season with a pinch of salt and pepper.
2. Melt the butter over medium heat in a large skillet. Add the minced garlic and sauté for about 1 minute, until fragrant.
3. Add the shrimp to the skillet in a single layer. Cook for 2-3 minutes on each side until they turn pink and opaque.
4. Pour in the lemon juice and zest, giving the shrimp a delightful citrus kick. Allow the flavors to meld for another 1-2 minutes.
5. Move the skillet from the heat and give the shrimp a final toss in the lemony butter sauce.
6. Serve the succulent lemon butter shrimp over a bed of steamed quinoa or a colorful assortment of sautéed vegetables.

RECIPE TIP: To enhance the dish's nutritional profile, use grass-fed butter with higher levels of beneficial fatty acids.

SUBSTITUTION TIP:
- For a dairy-free option, substitute the butter with olive oil. You can also use coconut oil for a unique tropical twist.
- Replace the lemon juice with lime juice or a splash of balsamic vinegar if you prefer a tangier flavor.

NUTRITIONAL INFORMATION PER SERVING: Calories: 220; Total Fat: 10g; Total Cholesterol: 235mg; Sugar: 0g; Fiber 0g; Protein: 25g; Sodium: 220mg; Potassium: 280mg

Experience rich flavors and nourishing ingredients with this Teriyaki Glazed Salmon. The combination of succulent fish, savory glaze, and wholesome roasted vegetables creates a memorable meal perfect for any occasion.

TERIYAKI GLAZED SALMON & ROASTED VEGGIES

✅ Servings: 4   ✅ Preparation time: 15 min   ✅ Cooking time: 25 min

- 4 salmon fillets (6 oz / 170g each), skinless
- 4 medium carrots, halved lengthwise
- 2 cups broccoli florets
- 1/4 cup low-sodium soy sauce
- 2 tbsp honey

- 1 tbsp sesame oil
- 1 tsp fresh ginger, grated
- 2 cloves garlic, minced
- 1 tbsp sesame seeds
- Sesame seeds and fresh oregano for garnish

1. Mix the soy sauce, grated ginger, sesame oil, honey, and minced garlic in a small bowl to create the teriyaki glaze.
2. Put the salmon fillets in a shallow dish and pour half of the teriyaki glaze over them. Allow them to marinate for about 10 minutes, turning once.
3. Preheat the oven to 400°F (200°C).
4. Line a baking sheet with parchment paper. Arrange the marinated salmon fillets on one side of the sheet.
5. Place the halved carrots and broccoli florets on the other side of the baking sheet. Drizzle with a bit of olive oil and season with salt and pepper.
6. Roast the carrots and broccoli in the oven for 20-25 minutes until tender and slightly caramelized.
7. During the last 5 minutes of roasting, brush the marinated salmon fillets with the remaining teriyaki glaze.
8. Once the salmon is cooked through and flakes easily with a fork and the vegetables are roasted to perfection, remove from the oven.
9. Serve the teriyaki glazed salmon alongside the roasted carrot and broccoli, garnished with sesame seeds and fresh oregano.

RECIPE TIP: For a touch of freshness, squeeze some fresh lime juice over the dish just before serving to enhance the flavors.

SUBSTITUTION TIP:
- Use coconut or tamari aminos instead of soy sauce to make this dish gluten-free.
- Replace the salmon with firm tofu or tempeh and use a plant-based glaze with tamari and maple syrup for a vegetarian version.

NUTRITIONAL INFORMATION PER SERVING: Calories: 370; Total Fat: 16g; Total Cholesterol: 80mg; Sugar: 14g; Fiber: 5g; Protein: 38g; Sodium: 600mg; Potassium: 1050mg

Savor the elegance of the Garlic & Herb Butter Baked Lobster Tail, a dish that epitomizes indulgence while staying true to the principles of the anti-inflammatory diet. The harmonious blend of garlic, herbs, and succulent lobster meat will make your taste buds tantalized and your wellness journey enriched.

GARLIC & HERB BUTTER BAKED LOBSTER TAIL

✅ Servings: 2   ✅ Preparation time: 15 min   ✅ Cooking time: 20 min

- 2 lobster tails
- 1/2 cup unsalted butter, melted
- 4 cloves garlic, minced
- 1 tbsp fresh parsley, chopped
- 1 tsp fresh thyme leaves
- Salt and pepper to taste
- Lemon wedges, for garnish

1. Preheat your oven to 375°F (190°C).
2. Use kitchen shears to carefully cut through the top shell of each lobster tail, splitting it in half while keeping the meat attached to the shell's bottom. Gently lift the meat and place it on top of the shell.
3. Combine the melted butter, minced garlic, chopped parsley, and fresh thyme leaves in a small bowl. Season the mixture with a pinch of salt and black pepper.
4. Brush the garlic and herb butter mixture generously over the exposed lobster meat.
5. Place the lobster tails on a baking sheet lined with parchment paper. Bake in the oven for 12-15 minutes until the lobster meat is opaque and cooked through.
6. While the lobster tails are baking, prepare a dipping sauce by mixing melted butter with a sprinkle of chopped parsley and a squeeze of lemon juice.
7. To serve, place the baked lobster tails on individual plates. Serve alongside the dipping sauce and lemon wedges.

RECIPE TIP: Pair the Garlic & Herb Butter Baked Lobster Tail with a light salad and steamed vegetables to create a well-balanced and visually appealing meal.

SUBSTITUTION TIP:
- Substitute the butter with olive oil or a dairy-free substitute for a dairy-free option.
- Customize the herb blend using your favorite fresh herbs, such as basil, rosemary, or tarragon, to infuse the lobster with unique flavors.

NUTRITIONAL INFORMATION PER SERVING: Calories: 380; Total Fat: 29g; Total Cholesterol: 165mg; Sugar: 0g; Fiber 0g; Protein: 28g; Sodium: 290mg; Potassium: 310mg

Enjoy the Tomato-Basil Pasta with Mussels & Shrimps as a delightful way to include seafood into your anti-inflammatory diet. The vibrant tomatoes, aromatic basil, and succulent seafood will transport your taste buds to a place of culinary bliss while promoting overall wellness.

TOMATO-BASIL PASTA WITH MUSSELS & SHRIMP

✅ Servings: 4   ✅ Preparation time: 15 min   ✅ Cooking time: 25 min

- 8 oz / 225g whole wheat pasta
- 1 lb (450g) mussels, cleaned and debearded
- 1/2 lb (225g) large shrimp, peeled & deveined
- 2 tbsp extra-virgin olive oil
- 1 small onion, finely chopped
- 3 cloves garlic, minced

- 1 can (14 oz / 400g) diced tomatoes, drained
- 1/4 cup fresh basil leaves, chopped
- 1/2 tsp red pepper flakes
- Salt and pepper to taste
- Fresh parsley, chopped (for garnish)

1. Cook the whole wheat pasta according to the package instructions until al dente. Drain and set aside.
2. Heat the extra-virgin olive oil over medium heat in a large skillet. Add the chopped onion and sauté until translucent.
3. Add the red pepper flakes and minced garlic to the skillet, and sauté for 1-2 minutes until fragrant.
4. Stir in the drained diced tomatoes and chopped basil leaves. Allow the mixture to simmer for about 5 minutes, allowing the flavors to meld together.
5. Gently add the cleaned mussels and large shrimp to the skillet. Cover the skillet with a lid and let the seafood cook for 5-7 minutes, or until the mussels have opened and the shrimp turn pink and opaque.
6. Season the seafood mixture with salt and pepper to taste.
7. To serve, arrange the cooked whole wheat pasta on plates. Top with the tomato and seafood mixture. Garnish with freshly chopped parsley.

RECIPE TIP: For an extra burst of flavor, drizzle a touch of extra-virgin olive oil over the plated pasta before serving.

SUBSTITUTION TIP:
- Use gluten-free pasta instead of whole wheat pasta to make this dish gluten-free.
- If mussels are unavailable, you can use clams or other seafood of your choice.
- Adjust the level of red pepper flakes to suit your preferred level of spiciness.

NUTRITIONAL INFORMATION PER SERVING: Calories: 380; Total Fat: 8g; Total Cholesterol: 120mg; Sugar: 4g; Fiber: 6g; Protein: 30g; Sodium: 520mg; Potassium: 650mg

Immerse yourself in the flavors of the Mediterranean with this invigorating Octopus Salad. Tender octopus, combined with crisp vegetables and a zesty dressing, creates a light and satisfying dish perfect for a refreshing meal.

MEDITERRANEAN OCTOPUS SALAD WITH REFRESHING DRESSING

 Servings: 4   Preparation time: 20 min   ✔ Cooking time: 1 hour

- 1 lb (450g) octopus, cleaned and tentacles separated
- 1 carrot, peeled and finely chopped
- 2 celery stalks, finely chopped
- 3 cloves garlic, minced
- 1/4 cup fresh parsley, chopped

- 1/4 cup extra-virgin olive oil
- 2 tbsp red wine vinegar
- 1 tsp dried oregano
- Salt and pepper to taste
- Lemon wedges (for serving)

1. Fill a large pot with water and bring it to a boil. Add the octopus tentacles and reduce the heat to a gentle simmer. Cook the octopus for about 45-60 minutes or until it becomes tender. You can check the tenderness by inserting a fork - it should easily go through. Once cooked, remove the octopus from the water and let it cool.
2. Once the octopus is cooled, cut it into bite-sized pieces.
3. Combine the chopped carrot, celery, minced garlic, and fresh parsley in a large bowl.
4. Mix the red wine vinegar, extra-virgin olive oil, dried oregano, salt, and pepper in a small bowl to create the dressing.
5. Add the cooked octopus pieces to the bowl of vegetables and drizzle the dressing over the top. Gently toss the salad to mix all the ingredients and coat them with the dressing.
6. Serve the Mediterranean Octopus Salad on individual plates or a large platter. Garnish with additional fresh parsley and lemon wedges.

RECIPE TIP: To enhance the octopus's tenderness, you can gently massage it with a bit of olive oil before cooking.

SUBSTITUTION TIP:
- If octopus is not readily available, you can substitute it with cooked and diced calamari.
- Customize the vegetables by adding bell peppers, cucumber, or baby spinach to the salad.
- Make it vegan by replacing the octopus with marinated and grilled tempeh.

NUTRITIONAL INFORMATION PER SERVING: Calories: 240; Total Fat: 14g; Total Cholesterol: 40mg; Sugar: 2g; Fiber 2g; Protein: 18g; Sodium: 340mg; Potassium: 400mg

DELECTABLE
Desserts

Experience the velvety delight of Avocado Chocolate Cream Dream – a dessert that's both heavenly and health-conscious. This treat satisfies your cravings while aligning with the principles of an anti-inflammatory diet, allowing you to indulge without compromise.

AVOCADO CHOCOLATE CREAM DREAM

 Servings: 2   Preparation time: 10 min   ✔ Cooking time: 0 min

- 1 ripe avocado, peeled and pitted
- 1/4 cup unsweetened cocoa powder
- 1/4 cup pure maple syrup
- 1/4 cup unsweetened almond milk

- 1 tsp vanilla extract
- Pinch of salt
- Fresh mint (for garnish)

1. Combine the ripe avocado, unsweetened cocoa powder, pure maple syrup, unsweetened almond milk, vanilla extract, and a pinch of salt in a food processor or blender.
2. Blend the ingredients on high until you achieve a smooth and creamy consistency. You may need to stop and scrape down the sides of the blender or processor a few times to ensure everything is well-mixed.
3. Taste the mixture and adjust the sweetness or cocoa level according to your preference. If you'd like it sweeter, add a bit more maple syrup. Add more cocoa powder if you prefer a richer chocolate flavor.
4. Once the mixture is smooth and well-blended, transfer it to serving dishes or glasses.
5. Chill the Avocado Chocolate Cream Dream in the refrigerator for at least 30 minutes before serving. This will enhance the flavors and allow the dessert to set slightly.
6. When ready to serve, garnish with fresh mint leaves. The mint adds a refreshing element and complements the rich chocolate flavor.

RECIPE TIP: For an extra boost of flavor and nutrients, add a sprinkle of cinnamon or a dash of ground turmeric to the avocado mixture before blending.

SUBSTITUTION TIP:
- Substitute honey or agave nectar for pure maple syrup if you prefer a different sweetener.
- Adjust the thickness by adding more or less almond milk, depending on your desired consistency
- Create a nutty twist by stirring chopped nuts like walnuts or hazelnuts into the avocado mixture before chilling.

NUTRITIONAL INFORMATION PER SERVING: Calories: 240; Total Fat: 14g; Total Cholesterol: 0mg; Sugar: 18g; Fiber: 10g; Protein: 3g; Sodium: 50mg; Potassium: 580mg

Cool down and uplift your senses with the Orange Turmeric Sunshine Sorbet. This refreshing dessert combines the tanginess of oranges with the health-promoting properties of turmeric, making it a perfect summertime treat that aligns with the principles of an anti-inflammatory diet.

ORANGE TURMERIC SUNSHINE SORBET

✅ Servings: 4   ✅ Preparation time: 10 min   ✅ Cooking time: 0 min

- 4 large oranges, peeled and segmented
- 1 tsp ground turmeric
- 1 tbsp pure maple syrup
- Fresh mint (for garnish)

1. Place the peeled and segmented oranges in a blender or food processor. Blend until you have a smooth and liquid consistency.
2. Add the ground turmeric and pure maple syrup to the orange mixture. Blend again until the ingredients are well combined and the vibrant color of the turmeric is evenly distributed.
3. Taste the mixture and adjust the sweetness by adding more maple syrup if desired. Remember that freezing can slightly dull the sweetness, so it's okay to make it a tad sweeter than you would prefer.
4. Pour the orange-turmeric mixture into a shallow, freezer-safe container. Ensure the layer is not too thick, which will help the sorbet freeze evenly.
5. Cover the container with plastic wrap or a lid and place it in the freezer. Allow the sorbet to freeze for at least 3 to 4 hours or until it's firm.
6. When ready to serve, use a sturdy spoon or ice cream scoop to scoop out the Orange Turmeric Sunshine Sorbet into serving bowls or glasses.
7. Garnish each serving with fresh mint leaves. The mint adds a fresh burst that complements the sorbet's citrusy and earthy flavors.

RECIPE TIP: Add a splash of freshly squeezed lemon juice to the mixture before blending for a more intense citrus flavor.

SUBSTITUTION TIP:
- Instead of pure maple syrup, you can use honey or agave nectar as a sweetener.
- If you don't have fresh oranges on hand, you can use store-bought orange juice, but make sure it's 100% pure and not from concentrate.
- Enhance the texture and nutritional value by adding a handful of chopped pineapple or mango before blending.

NUTRITIONAL INFORMATION PER SERVING: Calories: 70; Total Fat: 0.2g; Total Cholesterol: 0mg; Sugar: 16g; Fiber: 3.2g; Protein: 1.2g; Sodium: 1mg; Potassium: 291mg

Delight in the exotic flavors of the Mango Coconut Chia Paradise. This guilt-free dessert is a fusion of tropical goodness and anti-inflammatory benefits, making it a perfect treat for satisfying your sweet cravings while nourishing your body from within.

MANGO COCONUT CHIA PARADISE

✅ Servings: 4   ✅ Preparation time: 10 min   ✅ Cooking time: 0 min

- 2 ripe mangoes, peeled, pitted, and diced
- 1 cup coconut milk (full-fat, canned)
- 1/4 cup chia seeds
- 1 tbsp pure maple syrup
- 1/2 tsp vanilla extract
- Fresh berries (for garnish)

1. Combine the diced mangoes and coconut milk in a blender. Blend until a smooth and creamy consistency.
2. Transfer the mango-coconut mixture to a bowl and stir in the chia seeds, pure maple syrup, and vanilla extract. Mix well to ensure the chia seeds are evenly distributed.
3. Allow the mixture to sit for 10 minutes, letting the chia seeds absorb the liquid and create a gel-like texture.
4. After thickening the mixture, give it a good stir to prevent the chia seeds from clumping together. Taste and add more maple syrup to adjust the sweetness if needed.
5. Divide the mango-coconut chia mixture into serving glasses or bowls. Cover and refrigerate for at least 2 hours or until the chia seeds have fully expanded and the dessert is chilled.
6. Before serving, garnish each serving with various fresh berries. The burst of colors and natural sweetness of the berries enhance the tropical flavors of the dessert.

RECIPE TIP: Add toasted coconut flakes on top just before serving to enhance the texture and taste with a nutty flavor.

SUBSTITUTION TIP:
- If you're dairy-free, replace coconut milk with almond milk or any other plant-based milk of your choice.
- Swap chia seeds with ground flaxseeds for an alternative omega-3 fatty acids and fiber source.
- Customize the sweetness using honey or agave nectar instead of pure maple syrup.

NUTRITIONAL INFORMATION PER SERVING: Calories: 245; Total Fat: 14g; Total Cholesterol: 0mg; Sugar: 21g; Fiber 6g; Protein: 3g; Sodium: 10mg; Potassium: 362mg

Indulge in the Coconut Blueberry Chill Pops for a cooling and nourishing treat that embraces the sweetness of blueberries and the creaminess of coconut milk. These popsicles are a delightful way to cool down on warm days while staying committed to your anti-inflammatory journey.

COCONUT BLUEBERRY CHILL POPS

✓ Servings: 6   ✓ Preparation time: 10 min   ✓ Cooking time: 0 min

- 1 cup full-fat coconut milk (canned)
- 1 cup fresh or frozen blueberries
- 2 tbsp pure maple syrup
- 1 tsp vanilla extract

1. Combine coconut milk, blueberries, pure maple syrup, and vanilla extract in a blender. Blend until smooth and creamy.
2. Carefully pour the mixture into popsicle molds, leaving a little space at the top to account for expansion during freezing.
3. Gently tap the molds on the counter to remove air bubbles and ensure the mixture settles evenly.
4. Insert popsicle sticks into the molds and place them in the freezer. Allow the pops to freeze for at least 4 hours or until they are completely set.
5. To remove the pops from the molds, briefly run warm water over the exterior of the molds to loosen the popsicles. Carefully pull them out and enjoy the frosty goodness!

RECIPE TIP: For an extra burst of flavor, consider adding a small handful of fresh mint leaves to the mixture before blending.

SUBSTITUTION TIP:
- Use almond milk or another plant-based milk instead of coconut milk if you prefer a lighter option.
- Swap blueberries for raspberries, strawberries, or blackberries to create your fruit-filled variation.
- Replace pure maple syrup with honey for a different natural sweetener.

NUTRITIONAL INFORMATION PER SERVING: Calories: 125; Total Fat: 11g; Total Cholesterol: 0mg; Sugar: 8g; Fiber: 1g; Protein: 1g; Sodium: 5mg; Potassium: 83mg

Elevate your energy levels with these delectable Carrot Cake Energy Burst Bites rolled in coconut shreds. These bites are filled with the vibrant goodness of carrots and the earthy warmth of spices, making them a satisfying and nutritious treat that can fuel your day.

CARROT CAKE ENERGY BURST BITES WITH COCONUT SHRED

 Servings: 2   Preparation time: 10 min   Cooking time: 15 min

- 1 cup grated carrots
- 1 cup rolled oats
- 1/2 cup almond flour
- 1/2 cup chopped walnuts
- 1/4 cup dried cranberries
- 1/4 cup pure maple syrup

- 1 tsp ground cinnamon
- 1/2 tsp ground nutmeg
- 1/4 tsp ground ginger
- 1/4 tsp vanilla extract
- Pinch of salt
- 1/2 cup coconut shred (for rolling)

1. Combine grated carrots, rolled oats, almond flour, chopped walnuts, dried cranberries, ground cinnamon, ground nutmeg, ground ginger, and a pinch of salt in a large mixing bowl.
2. Drizzle pure maple syrup and vanilla extract over the mixture. Stir the mixture until all the ingredients are thoroughly blended.
3. Using your hands, roll small portions of the mixture into bite-sized balls.
4. Place the coconut shred in a shallow bowl. Roll each energy bite in the coconut shred until fully coated.
5. Place the coconut-coated energy bites on a plate or baking sheet lined with parchment paper.
6. Refrigerate the energy bites for at least 30 minutes to allow them to firm up.
7. Transfer the energy bites to an airtight container for storage once chilled. Keep them refrigerated for up to one week.

RECIPE TIP: The coconut shred adds a delightful tropical twist. For added crunch, toast the coconut shred lightly before rolling the energy bites.

SUBSTITUTION TIP:
- Replace almond flour with another nut flour of your choice.
- Swap dried cranberries for raisins or chopped dried apricots.
- Adjust the spice levels to your preference by adding more or less ground cinnamon, nutmeg, and ginger.

NUTRITIONAL INFORMATION PER SERVING: Calories: 90; Total Fat: 5g; Total Cholesterol: 0mg; Sugar: 6g; Fiber: 2g; Protein: 2g; Sodium: 10mg; Potassium: 85mg

Indulge in dark chocolate's rich flavors and the sweetness from blueberries with these delectable anti-inflammatory cookies. These cookies are perfectly chewy and subtly sweet. These cookies are a delightful treat for your taste buds and well-being.

DARK CHOCOLATE BLUEBERRY COOKIES

✅ Servings: 16　　　✅ Preparation time: 15 min　　　✅ Cooking time: 10 min

- 1 cup almond flour
- 1/4 cup dark chocolate chips (70% cocoa content or higher)
- 1/4 cup unsweetened cocoa powder
- 1/2 cup dried blueberries
- 1/4 cup pure maple syrup
- 1/4 cup coconut oil, melted
- 1 tsp vanilla extract
- 1/4 tsp baking soda
- Pinch of salt

1. Preheat the oven to 350°F (175°C) and put parchment paper onto a baking sheet
2. Combine almond flour, unsweetened cocoa powder, dark chocolate chips, dried blueberries, a pinch of salt, and baking soda in a large mixing bowl.
3. Mix pure maple syrup, melted coconut oil, and vanilla extract in a separate bow until well combined.
4. Pour the wet mixture into the dry mixture and stir until a dough forms.
5. Take spoonfuls of the dough and roll them into balls. Place the balls on the baking sheet and gently flatten them with the back of a fork.
6. Bake in the oven for ten minutes until the cookies are set. Keep in mind that they will firm up slightly as they cool.
7. After the cookies are ready, let them cool for a few minutes on the baking sheet before moving them to a wire rack for complete cooling.

RECIPE TIP: Add a pinch of ground cinnamon to the dough for an extra anti-inflammatory boost before baking.

SUBSTITUTION TIP:
- You can replace dried blueberries with other dried fruits, such as cranberries or cherries.
- If you're avoiding chocolate, use carob chips as a delicious alternative.
- To make these cookies vegan, use a plant-based sweetener like agave nectar instead of pure maple syrup and choose vegan chocolate chips.

NUTRITIONAL INFORMATION PER SERVING: Calories: 120; Total Fat: 9g; Total Cholesterol: 0mg; Sugar: 6g; Fiber: 2g; Protein: 2g; Sodium: 30mg; Potassium: 70mg

28-DAY MEAL PLAN

DAYS	WEEK 1	WEEK 2	WEEK 3	WEEK 4
MON	**Breakfast:** Rise-and-Shine Overnight Oats **Lunch:** Mediterranean Magic Anti-Inflammatory Salad **Dinner:** Lemon-Dill Harmony Baked Salmon	**Breakfast:** Fluffy Buckwheat Banana Pancakes **Lunch:** Brown Rice Sushi Rolls with Creamy Avocado and Crunchy Cucumber **Dinner:** Ground Turkey Quinoa-Stuffed Bell Peppers	**Breakfast:** Spiced Pumpkin Morning Cookies **Lunch:** Savory Tuna and White Bean Delight Salad **Dinner:** Rosemary-Citrus Grilled Chicken	**Breakfast:** Banana Walnut Creamy Smoothie **Lunch:** Crisp Cucumber Avocado Gazpacho **Dinner:** Crispy Herb-Infused Oven-Roasted Chicken Drumsticks
TUE	**Breakfast:** Berry Bliss Anti-Inflammatory Smoothie Bowl **Lunch:** Grilled Chicken and Avocado Delight Wrap with Herb Infusion **Dinner:** Ginger-Turmeric Stir-Fried Tofu and Veggies	**Breakfast:** Mango Turmeric Morning Lassi **Lunch:** Tomato Basil Elixir Soup with Creamy Beans **Dinner:** Seared Ahi Adventure with Sesame Ginger Glamour	**Breakfast:** Avocado Toast with Radish and Microgreens **Lunch:** Spinach and Strawberry Balsamic Salad **Dinner:** Garlic-Herb Elegance Baked Cod	**Breakfast:** Fluffy Buckwheat Banana Pancakes **Lunch:** Brown Rice Sushi Rolls with Creamy Avocado and Crunchy Cucumber **Dinner:** Ground Turkey Quinoa-Stuffed Bell Peppers
WED	**Breakfast:** Berry-Licious Chia Seed Pudding **Lunch:** Lentil Sunshine Soup with Turmeric Touch **Dinner:** Crispy Herb-Infused Oven-Roasted Chicken Drumsticks	**Breakfast:** Mixed Berry Parfait with Almond Granola **Lunch:** Cauliflower Couscous with Herb and Pomegranate Burst **Dinner:** Baked Lemon Garlic Delight Shrimp	**Breakfast:** Berry Bliss Anti-Inflammatory Smoothie Bowls **Lunch:** Grilled Chicken and Avocado Wrap with Herbs **Dinner:** Ginger-Turmeric Stir-Fried Tofu and Veggies	**Breakfast:** Mango Turmeric Morning Lassi **Lunch:** Tomato Basil Elixir Soup with Creamy Beans **Dinner:** Seared Ahi Adventure with Sesame Ginger Glamour
THU	**Breakfast:** Savory Spinach and Sweet Potato Frittata **Lunch:** Spinach and Strawberry Bliss Salad with Balsamic Symphony **Dinner:** Butternut Bliss Chickpea Curry	**Breakfast:** Green Goddess Breakfast Bowl with Avocado **Lunch:** Chicken and Vegetable Stir-Fry with Cashew Crunch **Dinner:** Black Bean and Sweet Potato Enchiladas	**Breakfast:** Berry-Licious Chia Seed Pudding **Lunch:** Lentil Sunshine Soup with a Turmeric Touch **Dinner:** Crispy Herb-Infused Oven-Roasted Chicken Drumsticks	**Breakfast:** Mixed Berry Parfait with Almond Granola **Lunch:** Cauliflower Couscous with Herbs and Pomegranate Burst **Dinner:** Baked Lemon Garlic Delight Shrimp
FRI	**Breakfast:** Blueberry Almond Flour Pancakes **Lunch:** Roasted Vegetable and Quinoa Symphony Salad **Dinner:** Shrimp & Cauliflower Rice Stir-Fry Party	**Breakfast:** Avocado Dream Toast with Radish and Microgreens **Lunch:** Savory Tuna and White Bean Delight Salad **Dinner:** Rosemary-Citrus Grilled Chicken	**Breakfast:** Savory Spinach and Sweet Potato Frittata **Lunch:** Savory Tuna and White Bean Delight Salad **Dinner:** Butternut Bliss Chickpea Curry	**Breakfast:** Green Goddess Breakfast Bowl with Avocado **Lunch:** Chicken and Vegetable Stir-Fry with Cashew Crunch **Dinner:** Black Bean and Sweet Potato Enchiladas
SAT	**Breakfast:** Apple Cinnamon Quinoa Porridge **Lunch:** Mediterranean Stuffed Zucchini Sailboats **Dinner:** Moroccan Quinoa Cauldron with Lentil Magic	**Breakfast:** Savory Spinach and Mushroom Omelette **Lunch:** Vibrant Asparagus, Tofu, and Carrot Stir-Fry **Dinner:** Herb-Marinated Grilled Chicken Caesar Salad	**Breakfast:** Blueberry Almond Flour Delight Pancakes **Lunch:** Roasted Vegetable and Quinoa Symphony Salad **Dinner:** Shrimp & Cauliflower Rice Stir-Fry	**Breakfast:** Rise-and-Shine Overnight Oats **Lunch:** Lentil Sunshine Soup with a Turmeric Touch **Dinner:** Rosemary-Citrus Grilled Chicken
SUN	**Breakfast:** Banana Walnut Creamy Smoothie **Lunch:** Crisp Cucumber Avocado Gazpacho **Dinner:** Garlic-Herb Elegance Baked Cod	**Breakfast:** Peachy Ginger Sunrise Smoothie **Lunch:** Greek Goddess Chickpea Salad with Feta **Dinner:** Grilled Chicken and Avocado Tacos with Fresh Salsa Sauce and Lime	**Breakfast:** Apple Cinnamon Quinoa Porridge **Lunch:** Mediterranean Stuffed Zucchini Sailboats **Dinner:** Moroccan Quinoa Cauldron with Lentil Magic	**Breakfast:** Spiced Pumpkin Morning Cookies **Lunch:** Greek Goddess Chickpea Salad with Feta **Dinner:** Grilled Chicken and Avocado Tacos with Fresh Salsa Sauce and Lime

GROCERY LIST

Creating a comprehensive grocery list for all 28 days of recipes is quite an extensive task. Still, we've organized the ingredients into categories to make it more manageable. Please note that some elements may repeat across multiple days, and you should adjust quantities based on your needs and preferences.

Proteins:
- Boneless, skinless chicken breasts (about 14)
- Salmon fillets (12 oz /)
- Firm tofu (28 oz / 800g)
- Shrimp (1 lb / 450g)
- Cod fillets (8 oz / 225g)
- Ground turkey (1 lb / 450g)
- Ahi tuna steaks (12 oz / 340g)
- Eggs (at least 20)
- Canned tuna (at least 2 cans)
- Canned black beans (30 oz / 850g)
- Dairy-free cheese (1 cup, optional)
- Greek yogurt (2 cups)
- Plain yogurt (1 cup)
- Feta cheese (1/2 cup)

Fruits:
- Mixxed berries (at least 4 cups)
- Apples (4)
- Oranges (4)
- Banana (7)
- Mango (2)
- Peach (1)
- Lemon (at least 4)
- Lime (at least 2)
- Avocado (about 10)
- Ripe pears (2)
- Pomegranate seeds (1/3 cup)

Vegetables:
- Mixed greens (16 cups)
- Spinach (about 8 cups)
- Kale (about 3 cups)
- Arugula (about 3 cups)
- Romaine lettuce (1 head)
- Bell peppers (assorted colors) (at least 7)
- Cherry tomatoes (about 4 cups)
- Cucumber (about 8)
- Red onion (3)
-
- Sweet potatoes (6)
- Broccoli (about 4 cups)
- Cauliflower (1 medium head)
- Zucchini (at least 5)
- Carrots (about 8)
- Red cabbage (1 small head)
- Asparagus (1 bunch)
- Garlic (at least 20 cloves)
- Ginger root (1 piece)
- Tomatoes (canned or fresh, at least 42 oz / 1200g)
- Onion (2)
- Radishes (1 bunch)
- Microgreens (1/2 cup)

Grains:
- Old-fashioned rolled oats (about 3 cups)
- Brown rice (about 4 cups cooked)

- Quinoa (about 5 cups cooked)
- Whole wheat bread (16 slices)
- Corn tortillas (8)
- Whole wheat tortillas (8)
- Buckwheat flour (1 cup)
- Whole wheat flour (1 cup)
- Rolled oats (1 cup)

Nuts and Seeds:
- Chopped almonds or walnuts (at least 2 cups)
- Chia seeds (at least 1 cup)
- Flaxseeds (about 1/4 cup)
- Pumpkin seeds (1/4 cup)
- Sunflower seeds (1/4 cup)
- Sesame seeds (1/4 cup)

Dairy and Non-Dairy:
- Unsweetened almond milk (at least 5 cups)
- Non-dairy milk (1 cup)
- Plain Greek yogurt (2 cups)
- Dairy-free yogurt (1 cup)

Pantry Staples:
- Extra-virgin olive oil
- Coconut oil
- Honey or maple syrup
- Pure vanilla extract
- Dried oregano
- Dried basil
- Ground turmeric
- Ground cinnamon

- Ground nutmeg
- Ground ginger
- Ground cumin
- Ground coriander
- Ground paprika
- Cayenne pepper
- Dried thyme
- Dried rosemary
- Dried sage
- Garlic powder
- Onion powder
- Rice vinegar
- Balsamic vinegar
- Dijon mustard
- Tamari or soy sauce
- Nutritional yeast
- Cornstarch
- Sesame oil

Miscellaneous:
- Ice cubes
- Fresh mint leaves
- Fresh basil leaves
- Fresh cilantro leaves
- Fresh parsley
- Fresh rosemary
- Pickled ginger
- Wasabi

Please keep in mind that this is a general estimation, and actual quantities might vary based on your preferences and serving sizes. Check the recipes for any specific measurements and adjust the list accordingly.
Happy cooking, and enjoy your journey to a healthier lifestyle with this anti-inflammatory meal plan!

RECIPE INDEX

Printed in Great Britain
by Amazon

33740755R00051